THE GOOD, THE BAD, AND THE UGLY
NEW ENGLAND PATRIOTS

THE GOOD, THE BAD, AND THE UGLY
NEW ENGLAND PATRIOTS

HEART-POUNDING, JAW-DROPPING, AND GUT-WRENCHING
MOMENTS FROM NEW ENGLAND PATRIOTS HISTORY

Sean Glennon

TRIUMPH
BOOKS

Library of Congress Cataloging-in-Publication Data

Glennon, Sean, 1966–
    The good, the bad, and the ugly New England Patriots : heart-pounding, jaw-dropping, and gut-wrenching moments from New England Patriots history / Sean Glennon.
        p. cm.
    Includes bibliographical references.
    ISBN-13: 978-1-60078-118-6
    ISBN-10: 1-60078-118-7
        1. New England Patriots (Football team)—History.   I. Title. II.
    Title : New England Patriots

GV956.N36G54 2008
796.332'640974461—dc22

                                                    2008012334

This book is available in quantity at special discounts for your group or organization. For further information, contact:

Triumph Books
542 South Dearborn Street
Suite 750
Chicago, Illinois 60605
(312) 939-3330
Fax (312) 663-3557

Printed in U.S.A.
ISBN-13: 978-1-60078-118-6
Design by Patricia Frey
All photos courtesy of AP Images unless otherwise indicated.

To my dad, the first and best Patriots fan I ever met; my mom, who could probably pick Tom Brady out of a lineup; and my son, Seamus, whose ear I plan on bending about the Pats' dynasty years for the rest of my life.

CONTENTS

FOREWORD

It didn't take me long after I arrived in Foxborough for the first time to figure out that I hadn't landed with one of the NFL's elite teams.

Well, okay, I knew that before I ever made my first trip up from Alabama.

I knew it because I had never even heard of the New England Patriots before the day they drafted me. Seriously. I didn't know who the Patriots were. I didn't know where they played. I was kind of disappointed when I found out the Patriots had drafted me. I had hoped I would go to one of the teams I had grown up watching. The Giants, maybe. My dad had played a season for the Giants. Or the Steelers, Cowboys, or Packers.

What I did know about the Patriots was that they had hired Chuck Fairbanks away from Oklahoma. I knew Oklahoma. And I knew Coach Fairbanks was a good coach. So that was sort of the salvation for me.

Then I got up there.

One of the first things I remember happening was a reporter asking me how I thought it would feel playing in front of 55,000 people every week. The idea was, "Hey, you're in the big leagues now." But what I was thinking was, *Wow, that'll be disappointing.*

At Alabama we played in front of 80,000 people every time. And when we played at Tennessee it was even more than that. You know, 55,000 people—that was what we got for the scrub teams that we played.

That was all right, though. I was still proud and happy to be part of the NFL. I had worked hard to get there. I was going to make the most of it. And I wanted to give my new team some support. So I went out to some stores looking for T-shirts, sweatshirts, hats—something that I could send back home. I went to Jordan Marsh and Filenes. I went to every store I could find. And I couldn't find one thing with a Patriots logo on it. Nothing.

Matter of fact, I never did find anything that year. I ended up buying a bunch of Celtics stuff to give to my family at Christmas.

That's kind of just how it was. The Celtics were *the* team in Boston at the time. It made sense; they were a great team, a championship team. And, you know, everyone up there always loved the Red Sox. At the time, the Bruins had a big following, too.

The Patriots? We were sort of the red-headed stepchild. We had some great fans, don't get me wrong. The people who supported the team couldn't have been better. But a lot of people didn't know about the Patriots, and a lot more didn't care about the Patriots.

Unfortunately, it didn't take long for me to discover that not caring about the Patriots started with our owner, William Sullivan.

If you were around during the years I spent with the Patriots, I'm probably not telling you anything you don't already know when I say I never really cared for Bill or his sons, Chuck and Pat. I didn't like the way the Sullivans ran the team. I didn't like the way they treated the players. And I sure didn't think too highly of the way they conducted themselves.

I didn't figure out right away that I couldn't trust the Sullivans, though. That took a few years. Figuring out that Bill wasn't interested in running a first-class football operation, on the other hand, only took a few hours.

I got a bad feeling the first time I got a look at Schaefer Stadium. It was small. It was ugly. And worst of all, it was cheap. It wasn't the kind of building in which you expected to find a serious professional football team playing.

The team facilities were even worse. When I first got there we had two taping tables, a whirlpool, a hydraulic machine, and an ice machine. That was it. We didn't even have a weight room. If you wanted to work out with weights, you had to find a health club.

That wasn't what I was used to. I'd played for Coach Paul "Bear" Bryant at Alabama and Coach Bryant was a guy who wanted to keep his players well. He had every rehab machine that was known at that time. Coach Bryant had the philosophy of if you couldn't go first class, don't go at all. To come from that philosophy to the Patriots was really kind of sad.

The conditions in Foxborough back then didn't stop me from enjoying what I was there to do, though. I always loved playing football. I can't say the same about the business aspects of dealing with the Pats.

A lot of fans know that Leon Gray and I ended up holding out at the beginning of the 1977 season. What most probably don't know, or don't remember, is that Leon and I shouldn't have missed one game that year, never mind three. We had a deal worked out with Coach Fairbanks during the preseason. But Bill and Chuck Sullivan forced Coach to renege; told us and Coach Fairbanks they couldn't afford to pay the fair salaries we'd agreed on. We negotiated in good faith. They pulled the rug out from under us at the last second. That's why we held out.

A year later, the Sullivans refused to honor a deal Coach had worked out with Darryl Stingley before he got hurt. Darryl only played in that preseason game in Oakland without a contract because he was told he could sign his new deal when he got back home. He was promised that it was all taken care of. But after Darryl ended up in a wheelchair, the Sullivans denied they ever had an agreement. That was unforgivable.

That's when Coach Fairbanks started looking to get out. It's why he ended up making a deal with Colorado before our season was over.

I would have walked away then, too, if I could have. But there was no free agency at the time. You either played for the team that had your rights or you didn't play at all. I was stuck.

When I look at the Patriots now, and I see how well the team is run under Robert Kraft—the facilities they have, the way they support the team and the coach—it makes me happy and proud, but I'd be lying if I said I never wonder what it might have been like to play for a first-class team like that.

But, you know, I don't want to give the impression that it was all bad. I played 13 seasons for the New England Patriots and I'm proud of what I accomplished there. I'm also proud to have played for Coach Fairbanks and to have been on the field with guys like Leon Gray, Steve Grogan, Steve Nelson, Sam Cunningham, and Andy Johnson, to name a few. Plus, I was fortunate to be coached by some of the best offensive line coaches in the business: Jim Ringo and Red Miller. Coach Miller gave me the foundation for my position and the game. Coach Ringo taught me the finer points of my position and the game, things only someone who had played as long as he did and at as high a level of performance could teach.

I don't think I could have played with a better bunch of guys. And I think the things that we went through brought us a lot closer than players are nowadays. We faced a lot of adversity together and it kind of bonded us as brothers, made us more loyal to each other. I wouldn't trade that for anything.

I'm proud to have had an opportunity to play in the Super Bowl. I'm proud, too, to have been a part of the 1976 team, which was without a doubt the best Patriots team I played with. We could have won it all that year. We probably should have.

The best thing about playing in New England? It has to have been the fans.

New England fans are some of the best fans in the whole wide world. They respect and they honor a blue-collar attitude, and that's what always mattered most to me. I worked hard to be the best left guard I could possibly be. And I respected the players around me who came at their work the same way.

I learned the value of hard work from my father, who grew up a sharecropper and earned everything he ever had. My father was a great man. The way I trained, the way I practiced, the way I played, in a lot of ways, was a tribute to him. My belief that it wouldn't be right to give anything less than my fullest effort—in everything I did—was one of the values he instilled in me.

The fans in New England always understood what that belief meant. Even in the years when the team didn't do well, they stuck by the guys like me and Grogan and Nelson who they knew would never give anything less than everything we had.

I think New England fans are still like that. I think real Patriots fans love Tom Brady not just because he's brought home championships, but because they know how he got where he is. Fans know Brady had to work for it—and work harder than most other star quarterbacks. They respect that.

I respect that, too.

I'm happier now, I think, than I've ever been to have spent 13 years with the Patriots. I see what the team has become and I feel good about it.

I look at Bill Belichick and I think he's the coach Chuck Fairbanks could have been under the right circumstances. I look at what these guys have accomplished and I think, in a way, they're honoring what guys like Gino Cappelletti, Jim Nance, Houston Antwine ... all of those guys who built the team did—and what all the guys I played with did.

And I think about the fact that Robert Kraft was a fan back in the days when I was playing and I think, well, maybe we can take some credit for what's happened. Maybe it was the way we played that got this guy, who has become this great owner, to get excited about a team that was always the poor relation of the rest of the professional sports teams in New England. Maybe, in part, we inspired him to do everything he's done to make the Patriots a first-class organization.

You can't ever shake the bad—not completely. And you can't erase the ugly. But when I think about how it's all worked out, I have to admit, it feels pretty good.

—John Hannah

ACKNOWLEDGMENTS

There are only two people I could possibly start with: my wife, Mo, whose advice and support have been invaluable and who's had to deal with me being even more obsessed than usual with football-related minutia; and my son, Seamus, whose early-morning visits to my home office and regular requests for wrestling matches (or whatever they should be called—he's allowed to wrestle me, but I'm not allowed to wrestle him) kept me sane and grounded. Thank you both.

Thanks, also, to everyone at Triumph, particularly Michael Emmerich, who brought me in on this project and put up with my sometimes obsessive, sometimes silly questions.

Thanks to Stacey James and the New England Patriots, and to Randy Cross and the producers of Sirius NFL Radio's *The Opening Drive*.

And thanks to everyone who shared their Patriots memories and their ideas, specifically Tom Glennon, Ken DeCoste, Don Fluckinger, George Lenker, and Scott Brodeur.

THE GOOD

SUPER BOWL XXXVI: THE IMPOSSIBLE MADE REAL

No matter what ever happens, no matter what anyone ever says, the greatest day in New England Patriots history will always be February 3, 2002. And the greatest moment in Patriots history will always be the moment when Adam Vinatieri's last-minute field goal split the uprights and turned the Pats into NFL champions for the first time.

In many important ways, the best years—even 2003 and 2004, when the Patriots would emerge as the first (and perhaps only) dynasty of the salary-cap era; even 2007, when the Pats dominated most of their opponents while pursuing a perfect season—can never truly compete with that single, incredible day, or with that one, perfect, unbelievable moment. Because that day was never supposed to happen. And because that moment, even as it took place (and for the slowest second in history just thereafter) was never what anyone, anywhere expected.

Super Bowl XXXVI was supposed to belong to the St. Louis Rams. And everyone knew it.

Everyone had known it since September 2001. The Rams were a team of destiny, a dynasty in the making. They'd been league champions two years earlier, beating the Tennessee Titans in a hard-fought Super Bowl XXXIV, a game most remembered for the fact that St. Louis stopped the Titans from forcing overtime with a defensive stop at the Rams' 1-yard line as time expired.

1

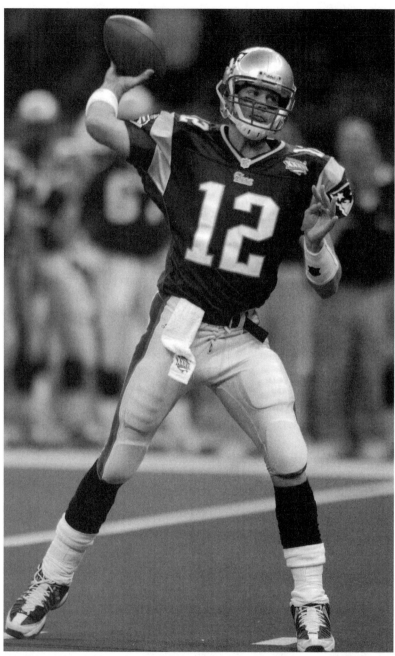

Patriots quarterback Tom Brady fires a touchdown pass to David Patten near the end of the first half of Super Bowl XXXVI against the St. Louis Rams.

The Rams took a slight step back in 2000, when defensive issues conspired with injuries to quarterback Kurt Warner and running back Marshall Faulk to hold their record to 10–6. They'd also taken an early bow in the playoffs, falling to New Orleans in the wild-card round. But the Rams had still managed to lead the league in scoring that season, posting 540 points.

The Rams began the 2001 season as a common favorite among experts to prevail in Super Bowl XXXVI. Their fast, efficient, and productive offense, dubbed the "Greatest Show on Turf," was back to full health. Their defensive problems appeared to be solved. It seemed nothing could stand in their way.

St. Louis hadn't disappointed during the regular season, either. The Rams won 14 games (including a week 10 victory over the Patriots at Foxboro Stadium that wasn't nearly as close as the 24–17 final score) and again led the league in scoring, putting up 503 points and becoming the only team in NFL history to score 500-plus points in three consecutive seasons.

The Patriots, on the other hand, had impressed no one heading into the season.

The Pats had finished the 2000 campaign, their first under head coach Bill Belichick, with a record of 5–11. And although Belichick clearly had set about remaking the team, there were significant questions about the way he was handling the project. Nearly one-third of the 2001 team consisted of unrestricted free agents and castoffs from other squads who had joined during the off-season (many of them willing to come to New England and sign on the cheap because their services weren't in high demand around the league).

It's fairly easy four Super Bowl appearances later to look at the 2001 season in retrospect and recognize Belichick and vice president of player personnel Scott Pioli's master plan coming together (easier still when you see it all spelled out in Christopher Price's book *The Blueprint*). But at the time, from an outsider's perspective, it appeared the team had a very long way to go. In fact, it looked as if Belichick, then known mainly for having compiled a record of 36–44 in five years as head coach in Cleveland, might be just another in the long line of coaches who had led the Patriots to near-mediocrity.

And the Pats didn't start changing minds early on.

They opened the season with a 23–17 loss in Cincinnati. The Bengals, by way of context, were on their way to a 6–10 finish behind one of the worst offenses in the league.

Two weeks later (following a weekend in which all NFL games were postponed due to the September 11 attacks) the Patriots struggled to a 10–3 loss to the New York Jets. Worse still, Drew Bledsoe, who had quarterbacked the team for eight seasons, suffered a serious injury from a fourth-quarter cheap-shot hit by Jets linebacker Mo Lewis. The injury would sideline Bledsoe for several weeks.

And while it might be romantic now to think that Tom Brady stepped in for Bledsoe and immediately turned the team's fortunes around, nothing could be further from the truth. Yes, the team won in Brady's first-ever start, beating the Indianapolis Colts 44–13, but the triumph was decidedly defensive. Brady mostly managed not to lose. In week four the young QB looked downright awful in a 30–10 loss to the Miami Dolphins, completing 12 of 24 passes for 86 yards and losing a pair of fumbles.

Brady's play remained inconsistent right up through the loss to St. Louis in week 10. But there were enough flashes of brilliance sprinkled in for him to begin building a strong following among fans and in the media. Brady had a presence on the field that Bledsoe lacked. And the stare that shot out from under his helmet made it clear Brady knew where he was going and he wasn't planning to let anyone get in his way.

More importantly, Brady had demonstrated an understanding of Belichick's offensive system and philosophy that Bledsoe had not. That spurred the coach to continue starting the second-year signal caller even after Bledsoe was cleared to play again starting in week 11, effectively benching a quarterback who'd signed a record-setting 10-year, $103 million contract extension the previous March for a player who'd been a sixth-round draft pick (an afterthought as far as fans were concerned). The team's record at the time was 5–5. It appeared as if Belichick had decided to start preparing for 2002. It looked like the 2001 Patriots were going nowhere.

Then the unimaginable happened. The Pats went on a six-game winning streak to finish the regular season, edging Miami for the division title and grabbing the number two seed in the AFC.

The Patriots beat the Oakland Raiders in an incredible nail-biter playoff game in which Vinatieri nailed a pair of clutch kicks—one to tie the game and another to win it in overtime—in a driving snowstorm. Then they traveled to Pittsburgh and beat a Steelers team that had made a show of booking its hotel rooms in New Orleans for the Super Bowl even before winning the conference championship.

The Pats won both playoff games through huge defensive efforts. They scored just one offensive touchdown in each contest. No one believed a team with that little offensive output could hope to keep up with the Rams.

So, of course, the Pats were 14-point underdogs going into the Super Bowl. In fact, the outcome seemed such a foregone conclusion that Rams wide receiver Ricky Proehl announced to NFL Films before the game, "Tonight, a dynasty is born."

Though Proehl had things turned around a bit, his statement proved prophetic.

The Pats came out tough and played aggressive, physical ball on defense, checking the Rams' speedy receivers at the line of scrimmage, disrupting their timing and their rhythm, dulling the razor edge St. Louis had used all season to slice opposing defenses to helpless bits.

The Patriots defense held the Rams to three points in the first half while putting seven on the board for New England. Halfway through the second quarter, cornerback Ty Law picked off a Warner pass intended for Isaac Bruce and returned it 47 yards to put the Patriots ahead 7–3.

Then a turnover just before halftime set up a Brady touchdown pass to David Patten. The Pats went into the break with a 14–3 lead over the best offensive team in football.

The Pats continued to shut down the Rams through the third quarter. Toward the end of the period, veteran cornerback Otis Smith picked off another Warner pass, setting up a short drive and a field goal that put the Patriots ahead 17–3.

It looked like the Rams might be done. But they weren't. St. Louis mounted a 12-play scoring drive to open the fourth quarter. That drive not only brought the Rams to within a touchdown of tying the game but also included a moment of classic Patriots heartbreak. Attempting to score on fourth-and-goal from the Patriots' 3-yard line, Warner coughed up the ball, which was picked up and returned 97 yards for a touchdown by safety Tebucky Jones. But the play was overturned because of a defensive holding call on linebacker Willie McGinest. The Rams got the ball back along with a new set of downs. Two plays later, the score was 17–10.

Just after the two-minute warning, St. Louis started a drive at their own 45-yard line. It took just three plays and 21 seconds of game time for Warner to tie the game with a 26-yard strike to Proehl.

As the Pats prepared to get the ball back with just 1:30 to play, John Madden in the announcers' booth opined that New England should play for overtime. Patriots fans watching the game booed their TV screens.

Overtime could only go the Rams' way. The Pats were getting the ball with time left in regulation, and they needed to do something with it. Right then.

When Troy Brown's kickoff return was stopped at the Patriots' 17, it appeared they might not get the chance. But Belichick and offensive coordinator Charlie Weis, not to mention the team, knew what fans knew: the only way to salvage the game was to play to win. And that's what they did.

"I don't agree with what the Patriots are doing here," Madden said as Brady brought the offense onto the field and started firing passes.

No one cared what Madden thought.

Operating out of the shotgun, with his deadly laser-beam stare guiding his throws, Brady methodically moved the Patriots downfield, completing five of seven passes for 53 yards. The drive included a spectacular 23-yard strike to Troy Brown that moved the Pats into field goal range with 21 seconds to play. After a final short pass moved New England to the Rams' 30, Brady walked

IN BETWEEN DAYS: THE 2002 SEASON

Only once in the years since Tom Brady assumed the job of starting quarterback have the Patriots failed to make the playoffs: 2002. It's hard to figure why. The Patriots operated without a spark all season long, struggling on both sides of the ball and appearing uninspired even in wins. Maybe it was a classic post-Super Bowl slide. Or maybe it was that the 2001 Patriots were greater overachievers than anyone realized. Maybe Bill Belichick and Scott Pioli's team-building program really shouldn't have produced a champion until later. Whatever it might have been, two championships later, it doesn't seem all that important.

calmly to the line of scrimmage and spiked the ball with seven seconds left on the clock.

"What Tom Brady just did gave me goosebumps," Madden said.

Then on came Vinatieri who had never missed a kick in a dome. He boomed the ball from the right hash mark 48 yards down the field and split the uprights. It was the first time a Super Bowl had ever been won on the last play. And the kick ensured that the game would forever be remembered as one of the greatest NFL championships ever played.

Most of the team mobbed Vinatieri. Brady and Bledsoe embraced on the sideline. And long snapper Lonnie Paxton, mimicking his celebration at the end of the divisional playoff win over Oakland, bolted to the end zone, slid onto his back, and made imaginary snow angels.

The crowd in the Superdome erupted. And back home Patriots fans paused in momentary disbelief, waited an endless second, sure it would all be negated by a late-flying penalty flag, then commenced celebrating.

Madden, too, was caught up in the moment.

"That's the way you should win a Super Bowl," he said. "I mean, they come in here against all odds. They were backed up.

They had no timeouts. And they drove the ball down and got in field goal position. That was a great, great drive."

It *was* a great drive.

It was a great game.

It was a great moment.

Not long thereafter Patriots owner Robert Kraft accepted the Lombardi Trophy and declared, "everyone in America is a Patriot." Brady grinned broadly as he was named Super Bowl MVP. And Pats fans, who were just beginning to let what happened sink in, realized that things would never be the same.

No one could have guessed the magnitude of the change that was afoot. But even if they could, they still would have recognized that there would never be a better day or a better moment in Patriots history. Not ever.

BACK-TO-BACK: A DYNASTY CONFIRMED

It all started with a woeful loss. Years later that can be difficult to remember. But at the start of the 2003 season, it seemed like the type of thing that would never be forgotten.

The Patriots had finished the 2002 season, their first campaign as defending champions, with a bitterly disappointing record of 9–7. Their nine wins were enough to land them in a three-way tie with the Miami Dolphins and New York Jets atop the AFC East. But the East was sending only one team to the playoffs that year, and the Jets came out ahead in the tiebreaker. The Pats stayed home.

Then, as if 2002 hadn't been frustrating enough, New England opened 2003 with an absolutely brutal 31–0 road loss to the Buffalo Bills, a team that featured former Pats quarterback Drew Bledsoe and, more important at the time, former Pats safety Lawyer Milloy.

Milloy had been released by the Patriots five days before the start of the season after refusing to renegotiate a salary that the team had determined was greater than his value. A seven-year veteran and four-time Pro Bowl player, Milloy had been popular with Pats players and fans alike. The decision to let him go was not well received. It confused fans and reportedly rankled players.

And the fact that Milloy signed with division-rival Buffalo just before the season started, then proceeded to have an outstanding game against his former team—he constantly brought pressure on Tom Brady, recording a sack and forcing one of the four interceptions Brady would throw on the day—didn't make things better.

Indeed, as the Patriots prepared to play the Philadelphia Eagles a week later, *Sports Illustrated*'s Peter King described the decision to release Milloy as a "dumb coaching move." And ESPN's Tom Jackson claimed damning insight into the mindset of Patriots players. "Let me say this clearly: They hate their coach," Jackson announced on *NFL Sunday Countdown*.

Pats players denied that there was any truth to Jackson's statement. And they went on to prove they could win without Milloy, defeating Philadelphia 31–10 in a game in which Eagles quarterback Donovan McNabb was sacked eight times and intercepted twice.

But 1–1 didn't really put the lie to continued assertions by local and national media that the decision to part ways with Milloy was bound to haunt the Pats. And neither did the team's outlook appear overly bright two games later. The Patriots' record stood at 2–2, the team having logged a hard-fought win over the Jets in Foxborough and a tough loss to the Redskins in Washington. Worse still, the Patriots were seriously banged up. Newly acquired linebacker Rosevelt Colvin had been lost for the season with a shattered hip socket. Linebacker Mike Vrabel and run-stuffing nose tackle Ted Washington both had suffered broken bones in the win over the Jets. And cornerback Ty Law, linebacker Ted Johnson, and wide receiver David Patten were on the injury report. It appeared another up-and-down season was under way.

That appearance proved more deceiving than most.

In a week five home game against the Tennessee Titans—a bruising team that had beaten the Patriots handily in a Monday night game in Nashville late in the 2002 season and was off to a 3–1 start in 2003—the Patriots dug deep, played 60 hard minutes of football, and came away having won and having reacquired the look of a champion.

It all came together late. The lead in the game had swung back and forth throughout the afternoon. Neither offense was making mistakes, and neither had committed a turnover during the first 58 minutes of play. Nor had either defense had much success keeping the opposition off the board. It looked like one of those matches destined to be won by whichever team held the ball last.

With 3:14 left to play, the Patriots scored on a 15-yard run by reserve running back Mike Cloud and went ahead 31–27.

When the Titans got the ball back, quarterback Steve McNair moved his team to the New England 40-yard line. And on the final play before the two-minute warning, McNair fired to wide receiver Tyrone Calico, who was being covered by a gimpy Ty Law. But Law was in better shape than McNair realized. He jumped Calico's route, made the pick, and toughed out a 65-yard touchdown return, cinching a New England win.

Generally, when sports fans tell you with the advantage of hindsight that they had a feeling about a day, a game, or a season, you can write it off as revisionist memory, a product of a strong desire to believe they never had a moment's doubt in their team. On this day it was different. Watching that game, Patriots fans really did know it was a turning point in the season. There was something special about the victory over Tennessee. The Pats played with toughness and ferocity they hadn't exhibited for a very long time, probably not since Super Bowl XXXVI. Watching them pull off that win, there was no mistaking that the team was back on track and headed for something big.

The Patriots never lost another game that season. They moved methodically through their schedule, finding ways to win every week, though never by any great margin until the season finale (a 31–0 win over the Bills in Foxborough). It was a game in which Lawyer Milloy was hardly a factor. It was also perhaps the team's second-most-satisfying win of the regular season, right behind a week 13 road contest in which they held off a second-half comeback by the hated rival Colts, stopping Indy at the goal line in their own building with 11 seconds on the clock to seal a four-point victory.

The Pats finished 14–2 and had home field advantage through the playoffs. After a first-round bye, they snuffed the wild-card Titans in a defensive struggle, a complete turnaround from the week five game in every aspect except the outcome. Then they punished the Colts in the conference championship, intercepting Peyton Manning four times (with Law pulling down three of those picks) and winning 24–14.

Super Bowl XXXVIII, in which the Patriots faced the Carolina Panthers, wasn't so easy. Though the Pats went into the game as favorites, the Panthers showed up to play and gave New England everything they could handle. In a weird parallel to Super Bowl XXXVI, Ricky Proehl, who'd migrated from the Rams to the Panthers in free agency, caught a game-tying pass (this time a 12-yard shot from Carolina QB Jake Delhomme) with just over one minute remaining on the clock.

And just like in Super Bowl XXXVI, the Patriots played to win it all in regulation, though this time they had help from an errant kickoff that sailed out of bounds and put the Pats at their own 40 to start their final drive.

FRONT OFFICE MASTERY: SCOTT PIOLI

Bill Belichick didn't transform the Patriots from doormat to juggernaut all by himself. From the start, Belichick's team-building success has relied on the aid and expertise of Scott Pioli, the Patriots vice president of player personnel. Pioli, like Belichick, believes in building winning teams by stressing versatility and value in assessing players. And he's consistently proven brilliant in his ability to evaluate draft prospects and veteran free agents, which is why he's a two-time winner of the *Sporting News'* George Young NFL Executive of the Year Award and the NFL Executive of the Year Award from *Sports Illustrated*. He's also been honored as NFL Executive of the Year by *Pro Football Weekly* and *USA Today*.

After five plays and four Brady completions, including a pair of 13-yard shots to veteran wide receiver Troy Brown and a 17-yarder to second-year man Deion Branch, the Patriots lined up for a 41-yard field goal attempt to win the game. And, once again, Adam Vinatieri was dead on in the clutch, putting New England ahead by three points with four seconds to play. A kickoff and a good stop later, the Pats were champions for the second time in three years. They were also the winners of 15 consecutive games.

They kept right on winning when the 2004 season rolled around, too, taking their first six games to post an NFL-record 21 straight wins. A loss to the Pittsburgh Steelers in week eight hardly slowed the team down. They rolled over their next six opponents, dropped a weird Monday night game to Miami in week 15 (the game was a low point in Brady's career, still remembered by fans for the fact that the normally unflappable quarterback visibly lost his cool in the game in which he threw four picks), then won their last two games to finish 14–2 once again. This time, however, the Patriots did not secure the AFC one seed; that honor went to the 15–1 Steelers.

Most of the Patriots' wins in 2004 came by more comfortable margins than those in the previous season, largely a result of the addition of Corey Dillon at running back. Acquired from the Cincinnati Bengals for a second-round draft pick, Dillon became the latest NFL bad boy to have his reputation altered and his career revitalized by joining the Patriots, much as had taken place with free agent safety Rodney Harrison a year earlier.

Dillon had gained a reputation as a malcontent in Cincinnati. He came to New England on the heels of an injury-plagued 2003 season in which he had managed only 625 yards and lost his starting job to Rudi Johnson. And some believed he was on the downside of his career.

In New England, however, Dillon became the model of a team player. He also had the best season of his career, rushing for 1,635 yards and posting 12 touchdowns. Most importantly, he took pressure off Brady, who never in his career had enjoyed the support of a marquee running back.

In a divisional playoff win over Indianapolis, Dillon posted 144 rushing yards, playing a major role in the Patriots' ability to hold on to the ball for nearly 38 minutes, which kept Manning and the Colts' high-powered offense off the field. The Pats routed Indy 20–3.

Dillon only carried for 73 yards a week later when the Patriots traveled to Pittsburgh, but his performance through the season and in the playoff game against Indianapolis forced the Steelers to respect the run, allowing the Pats to use play fakes and deceptions to rack up 41 points.

The defense sealed the deal, pressuring Pittsburgh's rookie quarterback Ben Roethlisberger throughout the game and picking him off three times.

In consecutive weeks the Patriots had shut down the league's top regular season offense (Indianapolis) and poured on the points against the league's top regular season defense (Pittsburgh).

The Pats went into Super Bowl XXXIX against the Philadelphia Eagles as seven-point favorites. They came out, once again, with a three-point margin of victory.

This time, however, New England didn't need any last-second heroics from Vinatieri to pull off the win. This time Vinatieri's winning points came a bit earlier. And the late heroics came from Harrison.

The Pats' offense struggled to move the ball early, but the defense stepped up, forcing Eagles quarterback Donovan McNabb to turn the ball over twice in the first quarter. The turnovers included a Harrison interception at the Patriots' 4-yard line. The teams traded touchdowns in the second quarter and again in the third. A two-yard touchdown run by Dillon put New England up by seven, and with 8:40 remaining, Vinatieri hit a short field goal to make the difference 10.

But McNabb moved his team to within three with a 79-yard drive ending in a 30-yard strike to wide receiver Greg Lewis with 1:48 remaining in the game.

The Pats went three and out but were able to pin the Eagles at their own 4-yard line with 46 seconds on the clock. Three plays later McNabb threw just too high for tight end L.J. Smith, allowing Harrison to swoop in, make a pick, and end the game.

THE COMPUTER WORE SUPER BOWL RINGS

The joke is that no one really knows what Ernie Adams does. The reality is that at least one person knows exactly what Adams's role is with the Patriots. As usual, though, Bill Belichick isn't saying much. Belichick's friend since prep school, Adams is reputed to be a walking computer, a man who has memorized thousands of hours of game film and who can instantly reference anything he sees on the field against virtually everything that's ever taken place in a game. Ever. He's also rumored to be able to analyze trends and predict future behaviors with stunning accuracy. Not a bad tool to have on hand when making halftime adjustments. If it's true. All anyone knows for sure is that Adams's title with the Pats is director of football research. And that the job has earned him three Super Bowl rings.

The Patriots had won their second straight Super Bowl, their third in four seasons—a feat that many considered impossible in the age of free agency and the salary cap. They had broken a 70-year-old record for consecutive wins. Moreover, in the 37 games since that 2003 opening day beat-down in Buffalo, they had gone 34–3. They were an unqualified dynasty, one of the best teams in pro football history, and surely the greatest of the cap era.

At the end of Super Bowl XXXIX, fans watched Belichick and his top assistants, offensive coordinator Charlie Weis and defensive coordinator Romeo Crennel, embrace and stand together soaking it in. By that point Weis already had accepted the job of head coach at his alma mater, Notre Dame. And Crennel was rumored to be the top candidate for the Cleveland Browns' head coaching position (he would take the job shortly after the Super Bowl). Fans knew, and the team knew, that the road in 2005 was likely to be substantially less smooth than it had been in 2004. But for the moment, that didn't matter. The Patriots were champions. Again. Again.

ONE TIMES 21 IS...

In Patriots talk—the language in which everything "is what it is" and there's no such thing as last week or next week, only this week—it was a series of 21 one-game winning streaks.

In the parlance of the real world, it was amazing: 392 days and 21 games without a loss. New England cranked out victory after victory, beginning in week five of the 2003 season and stretching through week seven of 2004. The 21 wins included 18 in the regular season and three in the 2003 postseason.

The 18 consecutive regular-season victories broke a record of 17 held by the 1933–34 Chicago Bears. The 21 including the postseason was unprecedented.

The final scores for each game in the streak:

- Sunday, October 5, 2003, vs. Tennessee Titans, 38–30
- Sunday, October 12, 2003, vs. New York Giants, 17–6
- Sunday, October 19, 2003, at Miami Dolphins, 19–13
- Sunday, October 26, 2003, vs. Cleveland Browns, 9–3
- Monday, November 3, 2003, at Denver Broncos, 30–26
- Sunday, November 16, 2003, vs. Dallas Cowboys, 12–0
- Sunday, November 23, 2003, at Houston Texans, 23–20
- Sunday, November 30, 2003, at Indianapolis Colts, 38–34
- Sunday, December 7, 2003, vs. Miami Dolphins, 12–0
- Sunday, December 14, 2003, vs. Jacksonville Jaguars, 27–13
- Saturday, December 20, 2003, at New York Jets, 21–16
- Saturday, December 27, 2003, vs. Buffalo Bills, 31–0
- Saturday, January 10, 2004, AFC Divisional Playoff vs. Tennessee Titans, 17–14
- Sunday, January 18, 2004, AFC Championship vs. Indianapolis Colts, 24–14
- Sunday, February 1, 2004, Super Bowl XXXVIII vs. Carolina Panthers, 32–29
- Thursday, September 9, 2004, vs. Indianapolis Colts, 27–24
- Sunday, September 19, 2004, at Arizona Cardinals, 23–12
- Sunday, October 3, 2004, at Buffalo Bills, 31–17

- Sunday, October 10, 2004, vs. Miami Dolphins, 24–10
- Sunday, October 17, 2004, vs. Seattle Seahawks, 30–20
- Sunday, October 24, 2004, vs. New York Jets, 13–7

The streak was finally snapped in a visit to the Pittsburgh Steelers on Halloween. The Patriots came out on the wrong side of a 34–20 score in that match. But that was okay in the end. A little less than three months later, the Pats returned to Pittsburgh for the AFC Championship and defeated the Steelers 41–27.

Of course, it wouldn't take long for the Pats' consecutive win records to be challenged—by the Pats.

The win over the New York Giants that completed the 2007 Patriots' historic 16–0 regular season was the team's 19th consecutive victory in a nonplayoff contest. (The 2006 team won its final three regular season games.) The Pats' chances of besting their 21-game win streak ended with their heartbreaking loss in Super Bowl XLII.

Records are meant to be broken. One game at a time.

THE BEST COACH SINCE LOMBARDI: BILL BELICHICK

If you like, you can choose to believe Bill Belichick's success as a head coach was inevitable. And at this point it could prove difficult to argue against you. Belichick possesses the best football mind of his generation. If you want to spin that into a contention that he was bound to deliver a bunch of championships *somewhere* at *some point*, you can do it without serious risk of injury.

You can even go the next step and conclude that the Patriots got lucky when Robert Kraft hired Belichick in January 2000. Maybe if Pete Carroll had fared better in his third year with the Pats—or if Kraft made a different choice to replace Carroll—Belichick would have ended up turning the New York Jets, or some other team, into perennial contenders and repeat champions.

You can believe any or all of that stuff if you want. You'll just be wrong is all.

The truth is that for all his football genius, for all the vision he exhibited in pioneering successful team building in the era of the salary cap, for all the wins, the streaks, and the Super Bowl championships, Belichick might never have emerged as one of the greatest head coaches in NFL history, perhaps the best since Vince Lombardi (though devotees of Chuck Noll, Don Shula, Bill Walsh, and even Jimmy Johnson might quibble with such a statement), had he not landed with the New England Patriots at the precise moment he did.

Belichick arrived in New England on January 27, 2000, some 23 days after he resigned as head coach of the New York Jets—a job he never truly held.

Belichick had been elevated to the top spot in New York according to a clause in his contract as Jets assistant head coach and defensive coordinator that automatically made him boss upon the resignation of Bill Parcells.

For a variety of reasons—not the least of which was that the Jets ownership was in flux, making any coach a potential lame duck walking in—Belichick had no desire to take over from Parcells, whom he'd followed to New York from New England three years earlier. As the Jets prepared to introduce him as their new coach, he handed team president Steve Gutman a sheet of loose-leaf paper on which he'd handwritten a terse kiss-off: "I resign as HC of the NYJ."

Belichick knew he was wanted in New England. He also knew Kraft's team was where he wanted to be. And the Patriots were willing to do what it took to hire him.

After the NFL ruled that Belichick was officially under contract with the Jets, the teams hammered out a deal that sent draft picks, including the Patriots' first-round choice in 2000, to New York in exchange for the right to sign the coach.

The situation awaiting Belichick with the Patriots was precisely the one he wanted. Belichick had been a head coach before, leading the original Cleveland Browns from 1991 through 1995. The experience had been less than ideal.

In Cleveland, Belichick had been forced to deal with regular meddling from owner Art Modell. He also had been put in the difficult position of having to coach the team for half a season after Modell announced his intention to move the organization to

Newly hired Patriots head coach Bill Belichick, left, shakes hands with Patriots owner Robert Kraft moments before the start of a news conference at Foxboro Stadium to announce Belichick's hiring.

Baltimore, an announcement that alienated the Browns' passionate fans.

Frustrated Browns fans looked at a team struggling through the season, looked at a coach whose personality has never been warm, and blamed Belichick for everything wrong with the team, including the pending move.

Belichick left Cleveland after that season with a 36–44 record and a bitter taste in his mouth. He wanted to be a head coach again, but only under the right circumstances. The Jets job didn't present those circumstances or anything remotely close to them.

In New England, however, Belichick could be sure things would be different. Kraft, who as a new owner had helped make a difficult relationship with Parcells untenable by meddling in personnel decisions, had matured over the three years since Parcells and Belichick left Foxborough. The Patriots' owner, an extremely intelligent business owner, had realized that the way to build a great team wasn't to try to impose his business beliefs on a coach, but to find a coach with as good a head for the economics of the league and the salary cap as he had for the game. Coaches with those qualifications were rare (they still are). But Kraft knew Belichick was one of them.

Kraft had also recognized his folly in allowing Belichick to leave the team in the first place. Though Belichick had only been in New England under Parcells for a short time, he'd forged an excellent relationship with the team owner. Kraft had considered offering the head coaching job to Belichick after Parcells skipped town. But he allowed his anger with Parcells to spill over to the Tuna's assistants and opted to bring in San Francisco 49ers defensive coordinator Carroll instead. Carroll got the job partly because he was the most un-Parcells-like candidate Kraft could find.

What Carroll was not, Kraft learned, was a great professional football coach. In his one season as head coach of the Jets in 1994, Carroll had achieved a record of 6–10. He reversed those numbers in his first season in New England, coaching the team Parcells had built and taken to Super Bowl XXXI a year earlier. But a year later the team's record slipped to 9–7. And in 1999 it dropped to 8–8.

Belichick had proven nothing as a head coach in Cleveland. But he came with significant football bona fides nonetheless. He owned two Super Bowl rings from his time as an assistant coach with the New York Giants under Parcells. And he had devised the aggressive defensive game plan that allowed the Giants to unhinge the Buffalo Bills' fast, high-powered offense in Super Bowl XXV, a game New York won 20–19. That game plan is on display at the Pro Football Hall of Fame.

When Kraft brought Belichick back to New England, it wasn't simply to coach the team, but to remake it. Belichick and his friend and protégé, personnel man Scott Pioli, had an idea of how to build a team that could succeed and endure in the cap era. Kraft's squad was facing a salary crisis. The Pats would have to trim $10.5 million from their payroll before the 2000 season began to get under the $62 million cap. It was time to try Belichick's new approach.

The move paid off. For Kraft. For Belichick. And for the Patriots. Though the team would finish 2000 with a record of 5–11, it would be only one more season before the Patriots would land at the top of the league, winning the first of three Super Bowls.

The quick turnaround had something to do with Belichick and Pioli's approach to team building. The new system emphasized drafting well above all else. But in the short term, it turned on two key factors. It disallowed any sentiment in evaluating players. No one kept a spot on the roster because he was popular with fans or teammates. No one was retained because of past contributions. And if Belichick considered a player overvalued he either reworked his deal or was shown the door. Similarly the system called for bringing in veteran free agents who could contribute without compromising the team's cap position.

Belichick's model was inherently holistic. Its central idea was that individual success grows from team success. It put no one player above his teammates. It spread out the money available under the cap more evenly than the star-oriented model used throughout most of the league.

It's largely because of that approach that the Patriots have been able to field perhaps the deepest team in the league season after season. In the NFL, where player losses due to attrition during any given season are inevitable, the Pats have succeeded in part because the second and third players at a position typically are closer in talent to the starters than is the case on teams that concentrate cap space on a few stars.

Quickly embraced by players (or at least the ones who stuck around), Belichick's team-first philosophy was put on display at Super Bowl XXXVI, when the Patriots insisted on being introduced as a team rather than as individuals. And neither time nor success has eroded the belief in Belichick's model.

During the 2007 season Tom Brady was pressed by WEEI radio morning host John Dennis regarding the notion that the team had been running up scores with the goal of humiliating opponents. If the goal wasn't to run up the score, Dennis wondered, why did Brady typically remain on the field late in games with the

Pats leading by 20 points or more? Brady's response, in part, was to question the idea that he should be allowed to make an early day of it while his teammates were asked to play through to the final whistle.

Belichick's philosophy also stresses versatility. Belichick expects nearly every player on his team to be able to function at a high level in multiple roles, particularly on defense, where players are asked to line up in different spots in different configurations as defensive looks change from game to game and sometimes from play to play.

Linebackers in Belichick's system need to be able to drop into coverage, rush the edge, and even to switch sides of the ball and function as tight ends or fullbacks on goal-line plays. Linebacker Mike Vrabel, a stellar pass rusher, has been used frequently as a tight end. Vrabel has recorded 10 career catches, all for touchdowns, including one each in Super Bowls XXXVIII and XXXIX. Similarly wide receiver Troy Brown has been pressed into service as a defensive back, sometimes for protracted periods, when injuries have taken their toll on the Patriots' secondary. And in 2007 wide receiver Randy Moss was called on to play DB in situations when an opponent was likely to throw up a Hail Mary.

That approach pays dividends both in ways that are expected—the Patriots' ability to show multiple looks on defense is often credited with rattling opposing offenses, shaking them out of comfort zones—and in ways that no one could anticipate. Possibly the most memorable play in Brown's career came in the Patriots' win over the San Diego Chargers in a Divisional Round playoff game in January 2007. After a Brady pass intended for Brown was intercepted by Chargers free safety Marlon McCree, Brown switched instinctually to playing DB, not only tackling McCree, but also causing a fumble that Brown's teammate Reche Caldwell recovered.

More than anything, the Pats' success has been a result of Belichick's unrivaled mastery of game planning and strategy. Belichick has a genius for identifying and exploiting opponents' weaknesses and for drawing up schemes that take away opponents' strengths.

SECOND BEST

The title of best coach in Patriots history is taken. Forever. Second best is probably not as obvious. Yeah, Bill Parcells brought the team back to life, but he finished with a record of 32–32. Some genius. Chuck Fairbanks, on the other hand, coached during a much more difficult era, had to put up with then-owner Billy Sullivan's numerous blunders, and still managed 46 wins to 39 losses. Fairbanks had an amazing head for the game. His defensive strategies are still an influence 30 years after he left the team. And had he worked for a better owner or had a little more luck, he might have actually been recognized for what he brought to the Pats and the game.

When he's really on, Belichick can often manage to turn opponents' strengths against them.

The coach has a particular knack for getting under the skin of star quarterbacks. Until the 2005 season, Indianapolis Colts quarterback Peyton Manning routinely posted his worst games against the Patriots. Ben Roethlisberger and Drew Bledsoe have also been victims.

There's no particular genius evident in recognizing that poor quarterback play tends to lead to losses, but Belichick has a unique talent for creating poor play by opposing QBs. He identifies not only what a quarterback does best but also what he likes to do most. And he implements a defensive scheme that forces the QB to play against his own instincts, setting him up to make deadly mistakes.

Belichick certainly has his weaknesses. It's arguable that the Patriots' failure to reach their fourth Super Bowl under the coach following the 2006 season is attributable, at least in part, to Belichick overestimating either his own abilities or the potential of his team-oriented philosophy. In the wake of wide receiver Deion Branch's extended salary holdout and eventual departure in a trade to Seattle, the Pats went with what was in essence a group of second and third receivers: Reche Caldwell, Doug Gabriel, and Jabar Gaffney. The absence of a true number one target put a huge burden on Brady and contributed to the team's ultimate failure in the playoffs.

Belichick's difficult relationship with the media, though at least to some degree a symptom of an unwillingness to suffer fools gladly ("I was at the game," he snapped at a reporter attempting to question decisions he made in a 2007 victory over the Miami Dolphins), also has proven problematic at times, particularly when critics have latched on to some reason to criticize the coach. It's hard to imagine that the ultimately meaningless Spygate incident, which dogged Belichick and his team throughout 2007, wouldn't have gone away quickly if it had involved a more popular coach like Tony Dungy.

But it's impossible to argue with Belichick's record. Since arriving in New England, Belichick is 91–37 in the regular season (86–24 with Brady as his starting quarterback), 14–3 in the postseason, and 3–1 in the Super Bowl. (The Patriots' pre-Belichick postseason record was 7–10, including a mark of 0–2 in Super Bowls.) That's an overall winning percentage of .724 with the Patriots. Even adding in his record with the Browns, Belichick's percentage only drops to .627.

Belichick's Patriots are one of three teams in NFL history to have posted consecutive seasons with 14 or more wins. And in 2007, they became the only team in league history to finish a regular season 16–0.

Belichick reportedly is under contract with the Patriots through the 2013 season. (Although the team is notoriously secretive about such details, ESPN has reported that the coach completed a deal to stay with the team through 2013 in advance of the 2007 season.) Time will tell what he can accomplish before he retires or his contract runs out. But there's little question that Kraft and Belichick both made the best, and most important, moves of their careers in January 2000.

TWO FOR THE HISTORY BOOKS

Sure, Bill Belichick has earned his reputation as a hard-nosed football coach—and maybe even his rep as a humorless individual.

But the truth is, Belichick isn't beyond having a little fun, even during a game. A dedicated football historian, Belichick has been known to cut loose and give players their chance to make a mark in the history books.

On New Year's Day 2006, at the end of a meaningless week 17 game against the Miami Dolphins, Belichick allowed veteran quarterback Doug Flutie to execute a drop kick for an extra point. It marked the first time the drop kick had been used on a scoring play in the NFL since 1941. And it provided a chance for Flutie, who at 43 years old was making his final appearance in a professional football game, to go out with a smile on his face.

The drop kick, in which the ball is dropped and then kicked as it hits the ground or as it bounces back up, was used in field goals and PATs in the days before the ball was made less round to facilitate the forward pass. With the less-reliable bounce of the pointed ball, the technique fell out of use. But quarterbacks of Flutie's generation were still trained to execute drop kicks. Flutie had asked Belichick for permission to try the technique in a game during the final three weeks of the 2005 season. And in that last game, he got his chance.

"I think Doug deserves it," Belichick said, smiling broadly, in his postgame press conference. "He is a guy that adds a lot to this game of football—running, passing, and now kicking. He's got a skill and we got a chance to let him use it, and I'm happy for him."

A year later Belichick once again gave a veteran backup quarterback an opportunity to make NFL history.

With the Pats leading the Tennessee Titans 33–23 with two minutes remaining in the final game of the regular season, Belichick pulled his second quarterback, Matt Cassel, in favor of veteran third QB Vinny Testaverde. The 43-year-old quarterback had played for Belichick in Cleveland and was with the Jets when Belichick was defensive coordinator there under Bill Parcells. He had been signed by the Patriots midseason to bolster quarterback depth.

Testaverde took over with New England at the Tennessee 36-yard line, moved the team downfield quickly, and with 1:45

remaining on the game clock, completed a six-yard touchdown pass to Troy Brown.

With that pass, his third of the game (and of the season), Testaverde extended his record run of seasons with at least one TD pass to 20. (In 2007 he'd make it 21 as a starter for the Carolina Panthers.)

Titans players objected to the touchdown, which they considered unnecessary. But Belichick simply smiled when asked during a postgame press conference about the decision to let Testaverde extend his record. "I wanted to give it to him," the coach said. "I think he deserves that."

THE BAD

THE INFERNO: SUPER BOWL XX

There are two broad categories of horrors a team can suffer in professional football. There's the kind experienced by every team—injuries that bring early ends to promising careers, apparent victories that slip away in the closing moments of big games, and seasons of futility and frustration when a team becomes painful to watch. And there are those that are unmercifully unique, that take up permanent residence in team lore, and that possess the power to evoke a squirm or wince from fans decades after everything surrounding them has passed into history.

Refrigerator Perry's touchdown in Super Bowl XX falls into that latter category—the singular horrors. If Super Bowl XX is a bruise on the flesh of Patriots history, Perry's touchdown is its most enduringly painful spot—though perhaps only for the frequency with which it's pressed.

It's not that the score put the Bears ahead 44–3 late in the third quarter. The Patriots had lost the game by that point. Another touchdown didn't make much of a difference.

It's not even the fact that Perry's one-yard dash put the icing on the Bears' cake. The 1985 Bears were one of the best teams in NFL history. They'd finished the regular season 15–1 and had shut out both NFC playoff opponents. No one, including realistic members of the Patriots' faithful, ever expected New England to emerge with a victory. In fact, had Chicago's future Hall of

Otis Wilson of the Chicago Bears hits New England Patriots quarterback Tony Eason in the disastrous Super Bowl XX in New Orleans on January 26, 1986.

Fame running back Walter Payton recorded the same score (which would have been the only Super Bowl touchdown in Payton's 13-season career), New England fans might actually have been able to stand back far and long enough to appreciate the moment.

What made Perry's touchdown so painful and so memorable was the fact that the decision to hand the ball to the 308-pound rookie defensive tackle with the ball on the goal line was a validation of the Bears' cavalier approach to the NFL's championship game. Chicago's players had spent the week goofing around in New Orleans, the Super Bowl's host city, while the Patriots prepared for the game of a lifetime. The Bears had made it clear that they never took their opponent in the biggest game of the season even remotely seriously. They mugged for cameras. They mooned press helicopters. They blithely insulted the virtue of New Orleans' female residents. And most of all they partied.

So when, with the game well in hand, Bears coach Mike Ditka called the handoff to Perry, it seemed as if he were saying, "You know what? We got it right. We didn't need to prepare for the Patriots. And, hey, while we're having fun, let's give the fat kid a turn in the end zone." Ditka and his team weren't simply putting an awful end to the Pats' Cinderella season, they were toying with New England in the process.

THE GOOD WITHIN THE BAD: SQUISHING THE FISH

If nothing else the Patriots came away from the 1985 playoffs having defeated the Miami Dolphins in the Orange Bowl for the first time since 1966. The Patriots dominated the Dolphins in the AFC Championship game. New England's defense took the ball away from Miami six times, recovering four fumbles and intercepting Dan Marino twice. And the Pats' offense pounded the rock all day long, logging 255 yards on the ground. The Pats came out on top by a score of 31–14, ending a powerful jinx and delighting fans in Squish the Fish T-shirts all over New England.

Worse still, Patriots fans watching the game knew that outside of New England and, perhaps, the home cities of Chicago's NFC Central rivals, virtually everyone in America loved seeing Perry crash into the end zone. Perry was a national celebrity, an unlikely hero on a team full to overflowing with hot dogs and media darlings.

You could love, hate, or love to hate Ditka and his swaggering, irreverent quarterback Jim McMahon. You could readily or begrudgingly respect the football genius of defensive coordinator Buddy Ryan, architect of the revolutionary and highly effective 46 defense. Likewise Ryan's players, notably linebacker Mike Singletary and linemen Richard Dent and Dan Hampton. And if you called yourself a football fan, you had to admire Payton, the veteran running back who was at the time the league's all-time rushing leader with 14,860 yards to his credit (better than 1,500 of which he gained during the 1985 season), even if you wished he'd done it with another team—*any* other team.

But the Fridge was a kid who made football fans smile. Perry hadn't run away from the game after Ryan looked at his 320-pound frame—a good amount of it plain old blubber—and declared that the team had wasted its first-round draft pick on him. Instead he buckled down, lost a bit of weight, and became a good (though never great) defensive lineman. He was a good-humored player. And when he started lining up at fullback on goal-line plays, everyone not playing the Bears was entertained. Perry scored three times during the regular season, carrying the ball into the end zone twice and catching one short TD pass. Most of the football-watching public wanted to see him do it again in the Super Bowl.

That didn't make things one bit easier from the Patriots' perspective.

That touchdown, the last offensive score Chicago would post in Super Bowl XX, erased what little remained of the respect New England had earned by becoming the first team to reach the Super Bowl by winning three road games in the playoffs. It ensured that the '85 Pats would be remembered not for their accomplishments during the season and the playoffs but for their failures in professional football's biggest game.

That may be fair, but it's painful just the same. Because the 1985 Patriots had a lot to be proud of.

Playing in their first full season under head coach Raymond Berry, the Pats had battled their way back from a rough start—they'd lost three of their first five games and appeared to be headed for yet another in a long string of disappointing seasons—to finish 11–5 and seize the fifth and final spot in the AFC playoffs. This despite the fact that injuries had forced a change at starting quarterback twice during the season.

Veteran QB Steve Grogan had stepped in after third-year man Tony Eason was injured in a week six game against Buffalo. Grogan led the team to a six-game winning streak that turned the regular season around. But Eason got the job back in week 12 when Grogan suffered a fractured tibia and sprained knee ligaments in a loss to the New York Jets. Eason quarterbacked the team to three wins in the final four weeks of the season, locking up the playoff spot with a win over Cincinnati in the final game of the regular season.

The team went on to win its first playoff game since 1963 in the AFC wild-card game (in the playoff system of the time, each conference's two wild-card teams played each other in the first week of the postseason), beating the New York Jets 26–14 at Giants Stadium. A week later, they toppled the AFC's top-seeded team, posting a hard-fought win over the Los Angeles Raiders. And in the AFC Championship, they broke an 18-game-old Orange Bowl jinx, beating the Miami Dolphins and denying young Dan Marino's bid to lead his team to a second straight Super Bowl appearance.

But the 1985 Patriots wouldn't be remembered for any of that (at least not outside of New England). Nor would the Pats be recalled as the team that scored the then-quickest points in Super Bowl history—with kicker Tony Franklin capitalizing on a Payton fumble to put the Pats ahead 3–0 one minute and 19 seconds into the first quarter.

Instead the Patriots would find their place in Super Bowl lore as the ultimate (in two senses of the word) punching bag for a Chicago team that had been destined to win the championship and that posted the league's second-ever 18–1 finish.

TIME HEALS SOME WOUNDS: THE SUPER BOWL SHUFFLE

It helps, if only just a little, to know that the '85 Bears are probably more widely remembered for their embarrassing pseudo-rap hit "The Super Bowl Shuffle," than they are for being one of the best teams in NFL history. "The punky QB known as McMahon" and his teammates may have their rings, but they also have to live with the images of themselves dancing awkwardly and rapping stiffly in what amounts to the one of the cheesiest expressions of self-conscious '80s schlock outside of Miami Vice.

They would be remembered as the team that finished the first half of the Super Bowl with minus 19 yards of total offense, the team with the only starting Super Bowl quarterback ever to fail to complete a single pass (Eason was 0 for 6 when he was pulled in favor of Grogan in the second quarter).

More to the point, the '85 Patriots would be forever known as the team that came out on the wrong end of one of the most lop-sided Super Bowls ever played (at the time, it was *the* most lopsided), losing 46–10.

"It will be many years before we see anything approaching the vision of hell that Chicago inflicted on the poor New England Patriots Sunday in Super Bowl XX," Paul Zimmerman wrote in the following week's issue of *Sports Illustrated*. Dr. Z was wrong—it would be just four years before the San Francisco 49ers would rout the Denver Broncos by a score of 55–10—but the point remains well taken. The Bears hadn't simply beaten the Patriots in the Super Bowl, they'd tossed the Pats and their entire season into an incinerator. And they'd had themselves a nice little party while they watched New England burn.

The Patriots had risen from nothing—which is to say a disappointing (to say the least) first 25 years as a team, a tumultuous 1984 campaign in which their head coach, Ron Meyer, had been fired midseason for being completely incapable of getting along with *anyone*, and a difficult start to the '85 campaign—to become AFC Champions for the first time ever.

Then in a single game the Bears had made the Patriots nothing once again. And in the moment when Refrigerator Perry posted the most famous six points of his career, there was little doubt that the Pats were going to remain nothing for some considerable time to come. That's the nature, the horror, of humiliation.

BETTER AND WORSE: SUPER BOWL XXXI

If the Patriots' second trip to the Super Bowl was less embarrassing than their first, it was also more heartbreaking.

Almost no one anywhere truly believed the Patriots had a chance to come out ahead in Super Bowl XX. But at least in New England there was a sense that the Patriots could pull off a victory over the Green Bay Packers in Super Bowl XXXI.

Sure, the Packers had been amazing through the regular season. The team, which for the fifth season was coached by Mike Holmgren and featured Brett Favre at quarterback, was the league's most dominant force. The Packers opened the season with a 34–3 dismantling of the Buccaneers in Tampa, closed it with a 38–10 beatdown of the Minnesota Vikings at Lambeau Field, and tore through many of the 14 games in between. They finished 13–3, the NFC's top-seeded team, and led the league in points scored (456) and points allowed (210) for a differential of 246 (an average of 15.4 a game). They were the first team since the undefeated 1972 Dolphins to lead the league in both points scored and points allowed.

The Packers also had dominated in the playoffs, topping the San Francisco 49ers 35–14 in the divisional round and the Carolina Panthers 30–13 in the NFC Championship.

But the Patriots were hardly the surprising AFC champions they'd been 11 years earlier. The Pats, who were in their fourth season under head coach Bill Parcells and with Drew Bledsoe starting under center, recovered from tough losses in Miami and Buffalo in the first two weeks of the season to finish 11–5 and win the AFC East. New England's offense, which managed just 20 points in those two early losses, came back to finish as the league's second-highest scoring unit, posting 418 points.

Bledsoe had the second-best season of his career, completing 373 passes (most in the NFL that season) for 4,086 yards and 27 touchdowns. And second-year running back Curtis Martin added 1,152 yards and 14 touchdowns (Martin had another 333 yards and three TDs receiving). Those would be far from career-best stats for Martin, but they were enough for him to finish second in the league in rushing touchdowns. Tacked on to Bledsoe's performance, Martin's made New England a recognizable force.

The Patriots' defense, though it finished the season ranked in the middle of the pack, had come on down the stretch. The D allowed an average of just 13 points a game over the final five weeks of the season, during which time it also boosted the team's giveaway/takeaway differential from +1 to +7, the seventh-best mark in the league.

New England entered the postseason seeded second in the AFC and had little trouble taking down their playoff opponents. Though Bledsoe and the offense stumbled a bit, the defense picked up the slack, carrying the Patriots to a 28–3 win over the Pittsburgh Steelers in the divisional round and a 20–6 victory over the Jacksonville Jaguars in the conference championship.

So while the Patriots may have been two-touchdown underdogs heading in to Super Bowl XXXI, the sense at home was that

BERRY THE BEARS

After Squish the Fish, there had to be T-shirts and (why not?) a song with a slogan for Pats fans to rally around for the Super Bowl. It may be hard to imagine that no one could have done better than "Berry the Bears" (with its delightfully clever play on coach Raymond Berry's name), but no one did. And so the rally song lyrics passed down to posterity: "Time to Berry the Bears. Try us if you dare. Now it's time to tear Chicago out of our hair." It's not "The Super Bowl Shuffle," but, really, what is?

Las Vegas had simply bought into the hype surrounding the storied franchise from Wisconsin. New England fans expected their team to make a much better showing.

And although the overall perception nationally was that the Pats were a Cinderella squad that couldn't hope to prevail against the league's top team, the home crowd wasn't entirely alone in believing.

"If I had to win one football game to save my life, I'd pick Bill Parcells to be the coach," Michael Wilbon wrote in *The Washington Post*. "The Patriots believe so profoundly in their coach that there's no way the Packers are going to win the Super Bowl by 14 points, if at all. Parcells is that good."

John Madden, too, said he expected New England to make it a game. Madden, who would call the Super Bowl for Fox TV along with play-by-play man Pat Summerall, offered his opinion during the buildup to the game. "I've been looking at New England on film the last five or six days, and the Patriots do a lot of things that impress me," Madden said. "I honestly think this could be one heck of a game."

There was hope. And in the end, that just made things worse.

Things started to unravel in the week leading up to the Super Bowl. Will McDonough reported in *The Boston Globe* that Parcells, whose strained relationship with then-new Patriots owner Robert Kraft was well established, had arranged to leave the team. McDonough's report was denied at the time though it turned out to be accurate. With the Pats headed for a championship showdown, Parcells was busy making a deal with the New York Jets.

If Parcells's plans (not to mention the time he reportedly spent planning his move) weren't enough of a distraction for the team, the media circus touched off by McDonough's report certainly did the trick.

By game day, it was clear that Parcells's loss of focus had infected the team. Unlike the Bears' defense in Super Bowl XX, which drew motivation from news that defensive coordinator Buddy Ryan would be departing after the game to become head coach in Philadelphia, the Patriots were obviously thrown by the shake-up at the top.

ANYTHING'S POSSIBLE: THE PATS TAKE THE LEAD

For a moment during Super Bowl XXXI, it wasn't just a matter of hope but actual belief. It appeared the Patriots really might beat the Packers. After Green Bay went ahead 10–0 early, the Patriots came back in style, scoring touchdowns on two consecutive drives to take a 14–10 lead. They looked like the Pats who had roared through much of the season. After that, however, the offense slowed down. And when Favre threw an 81-yard TD pass to Antonio Freeman, there was little doubt Green Bay had moved back in front for keeps.

That said, it would be wrong to claim that the distraction created by Parcells somehow cost the Patriots the game. The simple fact is that the Pats, as good as they were, simply weren't at the same level as the Packers. If the Patriots had played their best game, they could probably have kept Super Bowl XXXI competitive for a full four quarters and maybe even lucked into a win. That was about it. And they didn't even manage that.

The Patriots had their moments. Dave Meggett managed some nice kick returns. The defense made a few key stops. And Bledsoe completed 25 passes for 253 yards and a pair of touchdowns.

But Green Bay played a complete game. Favre passed for two touchdowns, of 54 and 81 yards, and ran for a third. The defense picked off Bledsoe four times. Future Hall of Fame defensive lineman Reggie White tallied a record three sacks, two of them coming on consecutive plays. And kick returner Desmond Howard became the first special teams player named Super Bowl MVP. Howard's record 244 total return yards included 90 yards on punts and 154 yards on kickoffs. His 99-yard kickoff return for a touchdown late in the third quarter sealed Green Bay's victory.

Favre's completion to tight end Mark Chmura on a two-point try following Howard's TD return wrapped up all scoring on the day. Green Bay won the game 35–21. The winning margin was precisely what Vegas had predicted.

No one was humiliated. But no one in New England was happy. Parcells was leaving. The end of an era had arrived earlier than anyone imagined or wished. And that era had ended in disappointment. Just like every era in Patriots history before it. It was going to be a long off-season.

THE WORST COACHING CHOICE IMAGINABLE: CLIVE RUSH OVER CHUCK NOLL

It bears noting that Clive Rush had been a part of one of the greatest upsets in NFL history less than three weeks before he was hired to coach the Boston Patriots in January 1969.

You have to talk about Rush's role as offensive coordinator of the Super Bowl III champion New York Jets if you want to be fair to Rush and to Patriots founder Billy Sullivan. Because after that, things get ugly very quick.

Or really, things get ugly a bit before that.

Sullivan's original first choice to replace Mike Holovak as his team's coach was Chuck Noll, who'd made a name for himself as defensive coordinator of the Baltimore Colts under Don Shula. It was a solid choice. Noll had been a defensive assistant coach with the Los Angeles/San Diego Chargers from 1960 to 1965, a period in which the Chargers took the AFL West title five times. In the 1963 AFL Championship, San Diego beat the Patriots 51–10. And in Baltimore he'd led a defense that gave up an NFL record-low 144 points in 1968 as the Colts put together a 13–1 season.

Rush, meanwhile, had been a losing head coach at the University of Toledo. The Weeb Ewbank-coached Jets team he joined in 1963 won just 29 of 70 games during Rush's first five seasons running the offense before going 11–3 in 1968. And while the Jets made a big splash by besting the heavily favored Colts in the Super Bowl, they did it with solid defensive play, not offense. The Jets won that game by a score of just 16–7. And quarterback Joe Namath, though he made headlines with pregame braggadocio and was named MVP, played unspectacularly, failing to throw a single touchdown pass.

Despite the fact that the outcome of Super Bowl III was the result of neither a failure by Noll nor a triumph by Rush, Sullivan believed he couldn't favor a coordinator from the losing team over one from the winning squad. So he rejected Noll in favor of Rush. And that decision not only doomed the Patriots to somewhere between 22 months and 32 years of futility, but it also set the Pittsburgh Steelers on the road to NFL history.

Noll, of course, would lead the Steelers for more than two decades. His Steelers would win four Super Bowls. His aggressive 4–3 defense, nicknamed the "Steel Curtain," would set the standard in professional football in the 1970s. And he would retire in 1991 with a career record of 209–156–1.

Rush, on the other hand, is probably best remembered for providing a bit of comic relief. Two weeks after he signed on as coach, Rush stepped up to the podium at a press conference held to introduce George Sauer Sr. as the Patriots' new general manager. Upon grabbing the mike, which wasn't properly grounded, Rush suffered a severe electric shock and began screaming. After the microphone was unplugged, Rush fell to the floor and lay there a few minutes before rising and quipping, "I heard the Boston media was tough, but this is ridiculous."

That's the highlight of Rush's tenure with the Patriots.

The lowlights include a record of 5–16 during his 21 games at the helm, a tumultuous relationship with virtually everyone he encountered, and a drinking problem that affected his job performance on the field and off.

Rush couldn't get along with his players. He couldn't get along with Sullivan. He lashed out at officials from the sideline to the point where he once drew two flags for unsportsmanlike conduct in a single game. He didn't simply court failure, he won her hand.

Rush's career with the Patriots ended on November 1, 1970, when he left the field during a loss (the team's sixth straight) to the Buffalo Bills.

Rush claimed to have experienced an irregular heartbeat. Observers claimed he had suffered a nervous breakdown. Either way he was gone two days later, just 22 months after taking the job. And Sullivan moved on to his next questionable coaching choice.

A HISTORY OF GETTING IT WRONG

Clive Rush is hardly the only questionable to poor coaching choice ever made by the Patriots. The team's selections over the years have included some coaches who turned out to be truly terrible along with a few who managed to achieve a certain level of mediocrity.

Lou Saban was the first coach of the Boston Patriots, leading the team in 1960 and '61. He was fired five games into the team's second season with a record of 7–12. Saban later coached Buffalo to two AFL championships.

John Mazur coached the Pats from 1970 to 1972. He resigned nine games into the 1972 season, a day after a 52–0 shellacking in Miami dropped the Pats' record to 2–7. He achieved an overall record of 9–21.

Ron Erhardt was in charge from 1978 until 1981, after which he was fired for being "too nice a guy" according to Billy

HOT AND COLD

Not every Patriots coach other than Bill Belichick, Bill Parcells, and Chuck Fairbanks has been a disappointment. Two were okay for a while.

Mike Holovak, coach of the Boston College Eagles through the 1950s, became the Boston Patriots' second head coach following Lou Saban's dismissal in 1961. Holovak was ultimately unsuccessful. He was fired after the team lost 10 games for the second consecutive season in 1968 and his overall record with the Pats was 52–46–9. But he did manage five winning seasons. And he led the Patriots to the AFL Championship game following the 1963 season. Of course, Boston lost that game to the San Diego Chargers 51–10.

Raymond Berry took over as Pats head coach after Ron Meyer was dismissed during the 1984 season and coached the team through 1989. Berry coached the team to 11–5 records and playoff berths in his first and second full seasons and led them to Super Bowl XX. Berry resigned after the team went 5–11 in 1989. He had a career record of 48–39 in the regular season and 3–2 in the playoffs.

Sullivan. His record was 21–28. Erhardt was an accomplished assistant with a great mind for the offensive game. He earned two Super Bowl rings as an assistant coach with the New York Giants. And his offensive schemes are still in use throughout the league today.

Ron Meyer annoyed players and fans from 1982 until 1984. He was canned eight games into the 1984 season for being an insufferable jerk who made virtually everyone who ever met him wish they hadn't. His record was 18–15.

Rod Rust is remembered as the worst coach in Pats history because of the horrid 1990 campaign. He was fired after "leading" the team to a record of 1–15.

Dick MacPherson is famous for being slightly better than Rust during his tenure, which lasted from 1990 to 1991. MacPherson was shown the door after the Pats finished 2–14 in his second season. His overall record was 8–24.

Pete Carroll coached the Pats from 1997 until 1999. He was let go gently after the 1999 season largely for the same reason he was hired: he wasn't Bill Parcells. (One way Carroll was unlike Parcells was that he managed to compile a winning record, 27–21.) Carroll has since come to be considered one of the great college football coaches. He has led the USC Trojans to six Pac-10 titles and one and a half national championships.

18–1 (THE EXACT WRONG ONE)

In the end none of it mattered. Not the first 16–0 regular season in NFL history. Not all the records set on the way. Not the hard-fought wins over Jacksonville and San Diego in the playoffs. None of it.

In the end what mattered was New York Giants, 17, New England Patriots, 14.

What mattered was that when the Pats made it to the big stage and had their chance to complete what could have been the greatest season in NFL history, they failed. The most potent offense ever was manhandled from start to finish in Super Bowl XLII by a Giants defense that played tough, smart football for 60 minutes.

And the Patriots D, though it played admirably, could never make the one big game-saving play fans had come to expect whenever the team got into a tight spot.

What mattered was that the big, bad 2007 New England Patriots, the first team in NFL history to enter a Super Bowl with a record of 18–0, fell to a Giants squad that had barely managed 10 wins in the regular season, that hadn't even won its division, and had tripped into the playoffs as the NFC's five seed.

Instead of making history as the uncontested greatest-ever NFL team, the Patriots made it as the team on the wrong side of the biggest title game upset at least since 1969—maybe ever. They let perfection float away, probably beyond their reach (probably beyond any team's reach) forever. The Pats may well play in another Super Bowl—possibly as soon as Super Bowl XLIII—but the odds that they'll get there without suffering a regular season loss or two on the way are incalculably slim. And that wouldn't be the biggest deal—perfection isn't really the goal—except that the team was so very close.

What made it all the worse—as if it could get much worse than losing one of the best Super Bowls ever played and destroying a perfect season all at once—was that Super Bowl XLII wasn't at all like the Pats' last heartbreaking loss. After New England dropped the 2006–07 AFC Championship to the Indianapolis Colts, you could look at the game, look at the team, and feel as if everyone should have known it was coming. The Patriots had left themselves exposed by going through a season without a legitimate number one receiver and they paid for it in the end. After Super Bowl XLII, all you could do was shake your head and wonder. Why? How? And whatever the answers may be, they'll never be enough.

The Giants were supposed to be victims, a final rollover on the way to immortality. They'd shown no one any reason to expect otherwise.

New York was a mediocre team at best throughout the 2007 season. Literally. The Giants offense ended the season ranked 14th in the league. Their defense ranked 17th. They sat firmly in the middle of the pack.

Patriots quarterback Tom Brady throws a pass in the second quarter of a November 4, 2007, game against the Indianapolis Colts. Despite a stellar 2007 season, the Patriots failed to deliver against the New York Giants in Super Bowl XLII.

The team had opened the season with a pair of losses and had rebounded by playing unevenly, winning by a touchdown here, a field goal there, while losing games by double-digit margins.

After a particularly brutal 41–17 home loss to the Minnesota Vikings in week 12—a game in which quarterback Eli Manning threw four interceptions, three of which were returned for touchdowns—the New York media declared Manning a bust and called for coach Tom Coughlin's dismissal. Even the home crowd saw no hope for the Giants.

New York's only close loss all season came in week 17, when the Patriots beat them 38–35 in the Meadowlands. They stayed competitive only by virtue of a long kickoff return for a touchdown and a late offensive touchdown that made the final score look closer than the game really was. Giants fans didn't realize that, however, because most of them weren't there. Having written off the season, Giants fans had been all too happy to cash in on their tickets, dealing seats to the Patriots-faithful eager to see New England complete its 16–0 regular season run (and to see Tom Brady and Randy Moss set touchdown records).

The Patriots' path to that week 17 game was something entirely different.

For New England, 2007 was a storybook season, complete with shining heroes, new and old, and rank villains who rose up only to be vanquished with all due speed.

It started with a week one victory over the New York Jets in Giants Stadium. New receiver Moss made it clear that reports of his demise had been monstrously exaggerated, making nine catches for 183 yards and a touchdown. Brady threw for more than 300 yards and three touchdowns. And the final score, 38–14, let the division rival Jets know who was boss and put the rest of the league on notice: the Patriots were the NFL's elite team.

And while it appeared briefly as if the Spygate incident—touched off by Jets coach Eric Mangini's decision to turn the Patriots in to the league for taping his team's defensive signals from an unapproved location—might derail the squad, a week two drubbing of the San Diego Chargers, again by a score of 38–14, made it clear that what was going on off the field wasn't about to affect what happened on it.

By the time the Pats wrapped up a 38–7 victory over the Buffalo Bills in week three, members of the national media were already beginning to talk about the potential for an undefeated season. On HBO's *Inside the NFL*, Cris Collinsworth, who had never been effusive in his praise for the Pats in previous seasons, became the first analyst of note to hold the '07 Patriots up as perhaps the best team in NFL history.

That kind of talk only intensified as the Patriots rolled over Cincinnati and Cleveland, then stomped on the previously undefeated Cowboys in Dallas, making a fool of Terrell "Getcha Popcorn Ready" Owens in the process.

The Pats failed to take heed of niggling complaints from assorted members of the local and national media that the team was "running up the score"—as if the Pats were preteen bullies

BELL'S TOLL

Upton Bell's single greatest achievement in pro football was being the son of an NFL legend. Bert Bell was a co-owner of the Philadelphia Eagles and later the Pittsburgh Steelers. He was NFL Commissioner from 1946 until 1959. And he created the rookie draft. Upton was a miserable failure as Patriots general manager from 1971 until 1972. He drafted poorly, traded poorly and, shortly after his arrival, accidentally made every player on the team a free agent. His late father, no doubt, would have been beside himself with pride.

insensitively humiliating the other children in the local Pop Warner league—as they manhandled the overmatched Miami Dolphins and rolled over the playoffs-bound Washington Redskins.

And no one charged the Patriots with anything other than being the best team in football after they went into Indianapolis for a midseason matchup of the last remaining unbeaten teams in the league—a game that was promoted as Super Bowl XLI½ and that drew the biggest TV audience of any regular season game in history—fought their way back from a 20–10 fourth-quarter deficit and walked away with a 24–20 win.

The Pats were challenged in week 12 by an aggressive Philadelphia Eagles team and nearly fell a week later on a rainy night in Baltimore. But they picked up the pace again in week 14, stuffing Pittsburgh Steelers safety Anthony Smith's guarantee of a win down his team's throat 34–13.

They dealt with Mangini in week 15, finished off the Dolphins in week 16, and headed back to Giants Stadium to close the season with a shot at the history books. And when all was said and done, though the Giants had given them a game, the Pats walked away with individual records, team records, and a perfect regular season in the books.

Throughout most of the season, the Patriots looked invulnerable. Pass rushers couldn't so much as make an appointment to see Brady. Although he was blitzed more than any other quarterback in the league, Brady took only 21 sacks while attempting 578 passes. He posted a league-best 117.2 passer rating, threw for a franchise record 4,806 yards, and completed more touchdown passes than any quarterback in league history.

When Moss wasn't open, Brady usually found slot receiver Wes Welker. When Welker wasn't available, he threw to wideouts Donte' Stallworth and Jabar Gaffney, tight ends Benjamin Watson and Kyle Brady, or tailback Kevin Faulk. And as defenses wore down, running back Laurence Maroney began to pick up yards and chew clock.

THE RECORDS

The Giants may have spoiled the Pats' perfect season, but no one can take away the multiple records set in 2007. At least not until someone finds a way to break them. Until then:

NFL records
- Passing touchdowns: 50, Tom Brady
- Receiving touchdowns: 23, Randy Moss
- Touchdowns by a quarterback/receiver pair: 23, Brady/Moss
- Players scoring a touchdown: 21 (ties the 1987 L.A. Rams and 2000 Denver Broncos)
- Team touchdowns: 75
- Total points: 589
- Regular season wins: 16
- Consecutive regular season wins: 19 (includes three from 2006; streak is still alive)

Franchise records
- Single-season passing yards: 4,806, Brady
- Single-season passer rating: 117.2, Brady
- Single-season completion percentage: 68.9, Brady
- Single-season receptions: 112, Wes Welker

The consensus was that the only way to slow down the Patriots offense was to pressure Brady. And with an offensive line that included three Pro Bowl players protecting the quarterback, that was virtually impossible.

The playoffs went largely the way the season had for New England. The Pats topped a much-heralded Jacksonville squad in the divisional round—a game in which Brady completed 26 of 28 passes (with one throwaway and one drop by Welker) to set a single-game accuracy record of 92.9 percent. Then they stifled the San Diego Chargers in the AFC Championship. Both games were tough, as postseason matches tend to be, but the Pats won by nine and 11 points.

And while their 37 points per game average in the regular season dropped to 26 in the playoffs, the Patriots still looked unstoppable heading into Super Bowl XLII.

The Giants looked better in the postseason than they had in the regular season but still not great. They won their wild-card game with Tampa Bay handily, but just managed to slide by Dallas in the divisional round and Green Bay in the NFC Championship.

New York was clearly a good team, and they were expected to put up a fight, but they certainly weren't supposed to win. Vegas liked the Pats by two touchdowns.

Then, on February 3, 2008, the teams took the field at University of Phoenix Stadium in Glendale, Arizona, and played a game that wasn't what anyone expected.

The Giants defense demonstrated throughout Super Bowl XLII why they had been the best pass-rushing unit in the league all season long. They challenged Brady from his first snap (an incompletion on a rushed throw to Maroney) until his last (a desperation deep pass to Moss on fourth down with 10 seconds remaining). They sacked Brady five times and flushed him out of the pocket on virtually every Patriots passing play all game long. And they did it without committing heavily to the blitz and exposing their secondary. Somehow the Giants found a way to break through the Pats' stout O line using only their front four.

Brady didn't have a horrible day. He completed 29 of 48 passes for 266 yards and a touchdown. And Welker tied a Super Bowl record with 11 catches.

But it wasn't a typical Patriots outing. The Giants held the Pats to one touchdown in the second quarter and one in the fourth. Fourteen points from a team that had averaged 37 during the regular season. That made the Patriots human—and being human made them beatable.

The Pats' defense had what might have been their best game of the season had one break gone their way. The D never gave New York's offense the chance to get comfortable. Early in the second quarter, cornerback Ellis Hobbs intercepted Manning deep in Patriots' territory, robbing the Giants of a scoring opportunity.

But although the Pats twice forced Manning to fumble at key moments, the Giants somehow managed to come up with the ball both times, once ripping it away from linebacker Pierre Woods at the bottom of a pile, once outracing Pats defenders as the ball rolled toward the sideline.

The D's most frustrating moments came during the Giants' final drive of the game.

After Brady led a masterful drive that put the Pats ahead 14–10 with just less than three minutes remaining, the New England defense found itself thwarted repeatedly in its attempts to end the game.

They failed to stop running back Brandon Jacobs from converting on fourth-and-one with 1:28 to play. An errant pass slipped through the hands of cornerback Asante Samuel with 1:15 on the clock. And on the next play, a third-and-five, defensive ends Richard Seymour and Jarvis Green somehow let Manning elude what appeared to be a sure sack. Manning launched the ball downfield, where wide receiver David Tyree caught it and pressed it between his hand and his helmet as he and safety Rodney Harrison tumbled to the field.

Tyree's catch will be remembered as one of the greatest nonscoring plays in Super Bowl history. It will be recalled in Patriots lore as the moment Super Bowl XLII was lost. Four plays later, when a Pats blitz left Hobbs isolated against wide receiver Plaxico

A LITTLE PERSPECTIVE

The Patriots may not be Super Bowl XLII champions, but they remain by far the dominant NFL team of the decade.

Only two teams have played in more than one Super Bowl since the turn of the century: the Patriots and the Giants. The Giants are 1–1. The Pats are 3–1. The Pats' 4–1 mark in conference championship games is similarly unequaled.

More impressive, the Pats dynasty has come about in an indisputable era of parity. In the seven seasons since 2001—when the Patriots made their first run to the Super Bowl—28 of the NFL's 32 teams have qualified for the playoffs. Only one, Indianapolis, has participated in the postseason as frequently as New England during that time. Each squad has made six postseason runs.

Burress, Manning threw the touchdown pass that decided the game.

The Patriots got the ball back but never really had a chance to do anything with it. A sack and three incompletions and their season was over.

They were 18–1. They were the team at the center of the biggest Super Bowl collapse in NFL history. They were better than the 1998 Minnesota Vikings and the 2005 Indianapolis Colts, but not as good as the 1984 San Francisco 49ers or the 1985 Chicago Bears.

And what does any of that matter?

What mattered was the heartbreak—on a level New England fans hadn't felt it in years. What mattered was starting all over again.

Bill Belichick was ready two days after the game to start planning and building for the 2008 season.

"The first thing is to go back and look at what happened in the season," Belichick told *The Boston Globe*. "Evaluate our team and our scheme and our players, and then we start moving into the team-building aspect and free agency, the draft, and personnel decisions and the playbook and stuff like that. All the things that we do to prepare for the off-season program, the spring camps, and ultimately the '08 season."

"It's pretty much over. Time to move on. I'm not going to sit here and dwell on anything good or bad. It's over. It is what it is."

And in 2008 it would be what it would be, which looked good when you gave it some perspective.

By February 5, ESPN's John Clayton already had named the Pats the early favorite to win Super Bowl XLIII.

"The Patriots should be no worse than 14–2," Clayton wrote in an ESPN.com piece. "Why? They have the easiest schedule in football. In fact, their .387 opponents' winning percentage for the 2008 schedule is one of the easiest slates in the modern era."

That was something.

And it seemed likely that by the first week in September it would be something big.

But as February moved on toward the Pro Bowl and beyond to the annual scouting combine, with free agency and the draft just around the corner, the might-have-beens still loomed large. And they still felt heavy. Something about them probably always will.

THE UGLY

THE WORST IN EVERYONE: THE LISA OLSON INCIDENT

It's not hard to identify the ugliest event in Patriots history. Not hard, because the incident left an eternal and indelible stain not only on the organization's history but also on the history of the NFL and all professional sports in America. It also led to actions that continue to stain the reputation and the collective soul of Boston sports fans.

Lisa Olson was a 26-year-old sports staffer for the *Boston Herald*, working the Patriots beat when, early in the 1990 season, she was sexually harassed by a group of players while attempting to conduct an interview in the locker room at Foxboro Stadium.

Women reporters in the locker room weren't unheard of at the time—they'd begun showing up in 1978, when a federal court ruled female journalists had to be granted the same access as their male peers—but they weren't particularly common. And there remained widespread confusion regarding legally required access to male sports locker rooms (so much so that the NFL had been forced to adopt an equal-access policy in 1985) and significant animosity among certain more neanderthalic athletes toward women reporters' presence. Women reporters continued to experience resistance by coaches and players in virtually every major professional and college sport.

Patriots tight end Zeke Mowatt ranked among the players who objected to seeing a woman in the locker room. And on

Boston Herald reporter Lisa Olson takes notes after one of the many Patriots games she covered. Olson was sexually harassed by several Patriots football players while conducting interviews in the team's locker room on September 17, 1990.

September 17, 1990, he decided to make his distaste for Olson known.

While Olson spoke with cornerback Maurice Hurst, Mowatt made his move. According to a report later prepared for the NFL by investigator Philip Heymann, Mowatt told offensive tackle Bruce Armstrong, "Look at her. She's just watching. I'm going to tell her about myself."

Mowatt then walked naked past Olson, climbed onto a scale located an arm's length from the reporter, and commenced to grab his genitals and wave them at her. "Is this what you want?" Mowatt asked.

As Olson attempted to maintain a professional demeanor, running back Bob Perryman joined Mowatt's act, standing behind Olson's back, gyrating his hips and making suggestive comments. Olson reported that the players, "dared me to touch their private parts."

Others, including wide receiver Michael Timpson (the only other player identified in the incident—largely because Olson refused to give them the satisfaction of taking her eyes off her interview subject), laughed and encouraged their teammates' disgraceful conduct.

When Olson reported the incident to her editors, the *Herald* approached the Patriots privately, asking for an apology and a meeting with team officials and the players involved. But the Pats dragged their feet. *The Boston Globe* heard about the incident and reported it, forcing the *Herald* to take the matter public. The national media picked up the story. And then things got even worse.

Victor Kiam, who'd purchased the Patriots from Billy Sullivan two years earlier, quickly made it clear that he grasped neither the enormity of the assault committed by his employees in his place of business nor the scope of the PR disaster the incident had created for his team and the league alike. Kiam didn't merely fail to launch an immediate investigation into what happened with Olson. He didn't simply fail to remedy the matter. He actually found a way to escalate the situation. He called Olson a "classic bitch" in earshot of reporters and told the *Herald*, in effect, that the incident was the paper's fault.

TAKING IT OUT ON TERRY

Robert Kraft wasn't the only person who was lashed out at during Bill Parcells's season-long temper tantrum over the decision to draft Terry Glenn. The rookie receiver also felt his coach's wrath. Though Glenn had an outstanding rookie season by any standard—catching 90 passes for 1,132 yards and six touchdowns—he was subjected to harsh treatment by Parcells throughout the year. Asked by reporters how Glenn was doing recovering from a minor injury, Parcells responded, "She's coming along," a comment that drew a strong rebuke from Kraft and caused many to wonder, if only briefly, how much had really changed since the Lisa Olson incident.

"I can't disagree with the players' actions," Kiam told the *Herald*, sounding as if he actually intended to pour fuel on the fire. "Your paper is asking for trouble by sending a female reporter to cover the team."

The league, among others, disagreed with Kiam's conclusion.

Commissioner Paul Tagliabue ordered an investigation into the incident and asked Heymann, a former Watergate prosecutor, to serve as special counsel and lead the probe. The move came as no real surprise, given both the image consciousness that had helped turn the NFL into America's premier professional sports entity and the fact that the league had only five years earlier made a point of instructing teams to welcome women reporters into their locker rooms.

Heymann and his team spent months interviewing Patriots players, coaches, and officials, as well as Olson herself, and prepared a 60-page report on the incident that concluded that Olson's allegations against Mowatt, Perryman, and Timpson were accurate.

In a letter to Kiam, Tagliabue said the incident "included a mix of misconduct, insensitivity, misstatements, and other inappropriate actions," and labeled the affair "damaging to the league and others."

The commissioner fined Mowatt $12,500, Perryman and Timpson $5,000 each, and the team $50,000.

The league also adopted a policy of training new players how to interact with the media, including instruction on proper behavior toward male and female reporters in the locker room.

What the league couldn't do was control the behavior of certain boorish fans who made the Olson incident even worse by blaming the victim for the crime.

Less than two weeks after initial reports of the assault broke, fans at a game against the New York Jets in Foxborough took to chanting Olson's name while tossing around an inflatable sex doll in front of the press box.

Olson estimated she received more than 100 obscene phone calls and more than 250 pieces of hate mail. The mail, she said later, included "depictions of rape scenes and horrible, horrible things."

The tires on Olson's car were slashed and a note left behind warning, "Next time it will be your throat." Olson's apartment was broken into and the words "leave Boston or die" written on a wall. "Classic bitch" was spray painted on the front of the victim's apartment building.

Olson continued to be hounded by fans even after she gave up covering the Patriots and moved to the Celtics beat. And again when she switched to covering the Bruins. In the end she had to leave town (she actually left the country, moving to Australia) to escape the onslaught of ignorant louts determined not to let her professional and personal nightmare come to an end.

Years later, with Kiam long gone from the picture and the team's current ownership and management committed to a model of personnel assessment in which character counts, it sometimes seems hard to imagine that the Patriots organization once stood at the center of such a firestorm and administered such a blow to the NFL's reputation. But it did. In its lowest moment. And in their own lowest moment, fans made things worse. The truth can be hard to live with, but it's the truth just the same: the stain may fade, but it will never disappear.

BETRAYAL: THE TUNA JUMPS SHIP

There are two things no Patriots fan will ever forget about Bill Parcells. The good one is that he transformed a franchise that had become the NFL's biggest joke into a respectable professional football organization. The bad one, which entirely and irreversibly trumps the good, is that he left the team in the lurch on the eve of what at the time was the biggest game in its history.

You can argue that the story of Parcells's departure from New England after four seasons as head coach is more complicated than that. And you'd be right. The rift between Parcells and the team had been growing since Robert Kraft bought the Patriots from James Busch Orthwein in 1994. Beloved though Kraft may be by Patriots fans, there's no pretending he wasn't at least partially responsible for his coach's decision to pull up stakes in Foxborough to return to familiar, and at least in one sense greener, pastures with the New York Jets.

But the story's denouement is decidedly simple nonetheless: the Patriots went into Super Bowl XXXI effectively rudderless and were promptly sunk by the Green Bay Packers.

Parcells, of course, wasn't technically at fault for the Patriots' second Super Bowl loss. The 1996 Packers were a great football team that was favored by two touchdowns well before the Big Tuna's plan to ditch his team became public. But more than a decade later, there remains little doubt that the coach failed to fulfill his fundamental duties to his team. In the weeks and days before the league championship, while he should have been hard at work on the game plan that might have led his squad to victory over a high-powered opponent—a feat he'd managed before, leading the New York Giants to victory over the favored Buffalo Bills in Super Bowl XXV—Parcells busied himself with lining up his next job and planning his escape.

Such blatant dereliction of duty by another coach might have been enough to derail the pending move and to destroy his reputation and possibly his career. That there was never so much as a hint of such a fate befalling Parcells likely is attributable to his considerable ability as a football coach and to his larger-than-life persona, both of which had been responsible for bringing Parcells to the Patriots in the first place.

Or, really, in the second place.

When Parcells was hired by Orthwein to take over as New England's head coach in January 1993, it marked a return to the team. Parcells had served as the Patriots' linebackers coach under Ron Erhardt in 1980.

It was in New England that Parcells had acquired his nickname, the Tuna—later Big Tuna—given to him after he told

Patriots coach Bill Parcells walks on the sideline after Super Bowl XXXI at the Superdome in New Orleans, where the Green Bay Packers defeated the Patriots 35–21. Parcells was widely criticized for making plans to leave the team on the eve of the game.

THE SETTLEMENT

When it became clear that the New York Jets couldn't hire Bill Parcells as their head coach without the Patriots' consent (which meant providing compensation), New York became creative, installing Bill Belichick as head coach and placing Parcells in an advisory role. No one was stupid enough to fall for the move, however, and the Jets were finally forced to surrender a first-round draft pick and three later-round picks to the Patriots in exchange for the right to hire Parcells. Of course, the Jets would get their due in draft picks a few years later when Belichick ditched them to return to New England.

players trying to pull a fast one on him, "You must think I'm Charlie the Tuna."

No one was joking when Parcells ended a brief retirement from coaching to take over the Patriots. The arrival of a two-time Super Bowl champion coach in New England represented the first indisputably sound coaching decision the team ever made (even those coaches who had worked out in the past were unknowns coming in) and also resulted in an instant change in way the team was perceived nationally. After the three horrible seasons that had followed the Lisa Olson debacle, the Patriots were viewed as a team on the ascent and worthy of serious consideration.

Three months after hiring Parcells, the Patriots made Washington State quarterback Drew Bledsoe the first overall pick of the 1993 NFL draft. The team had new leaders in place on the field and on the sideline. There was excitement. There was energy. And for the first time in forever there was real, if tempered, optimism regarding the team's future. It was a good time to be a Patriots fan.

The Pats finished the 1993 season with a 5–11 record, not much to boast about. But the team was improving. The Patriots were focused on the fundamentals, and the building blocks of good football were being put in place. That was enough to demonstrate to fans, the media, and the league that the team was indeed on the right track.

A year later the team had a new owner in Kraft. The dreadful expectation that Orthwein eventually would move the team to St. Louis was gone. When you considered the Patriots, there was little to consider other than football.

The Pats rallied from a 3–6 start to win their final seven games and qualify for the postseason for the first time in eight years. Although they lost to the Cleveland Browns in the wild card round, no one much cared. Things were looking up.

The team took a step back in 1995, going 6–10, but came on strong in 1996, winning 11 games, capturing the AFC East title, and battling through the playoffs to the Super Bowl.

While the Patriots were cruising through the '96 season, however, Parcells's relationship with Kraft was falling apart.

Kraft, a Patriots fan for decades before he bought the team, cared deeply about the team. But he was also a successful business-man who had bucked conventional wisdom and the counsel of his closest business advisors in paying $172 million for the Patriots (then the highest amount ever paid for an NFL team). He wanted to have a voice in managing his team. He didn't see any reason why he shouldn't have a voice in managing his invest-ment. He insisted on being kept informed of what was happening with the team. And particularly in light of the introduction of the salary cap in 1994, he wanted to be involved in matters regarding player compensation.

That level of owner involvement didn't sit well with Parcells, who was less than pleased by the Mara family's role in day-to-day operations of the Giants at the end of his tenure in East Rutherford. Parcells had returned to the NFL with the Patriots at least partly because Orthwein had promised him the authority to run the team his way. A man who has never been famous for his humility, the Tuna believed his football credentials were suffi-ciently established that he didn't need his new boss—not a football guy, just a fan with an overflowing bank account—looking over his shoulder.

The relationship between Parcells and Kraft deteriorated during their first two seasons together. It fell apart well in advance of their third and last.

Heading into the 1996 NFL draft, in which the Patriots would pick seventh, Parcells was intent on using his first-round pick on a lineman to shore up his defense, which had surrendered more points than all but five teams during the disappointing 1995 season. Kraft overruled the coach, however, and the team made Ohio State wideout Terry Glenn its top pick.

The meddling itself was more than Parcells could tolerate.

"It's just like a friend of mine told me," Parcells would say in a press conference nine months later. "If they want you to cook the dinner, at least they ought to let you shop for some of the groceries."

But the Glenn decision wasn't the end of the outrage. Kraft compounded the damage done in overruling his proud coach by explaining the pick to the media thusly: "There's a new sheriff in town."

The coach would later reveal in *Parcells, an Autobiography* that he was so angry he nearly walked out on the team a week after the draft. He only stayed, he said, because he didn't want to go out on a losing season.

BUFFALOED: CHUCK FAIRBANKS

Bill Parcells wasn't the first Patriots coach to put his next career move ahead of the team's best interests. Chuck Fairbanks's six seasons as New England's head coach came to a close in 1978 after it was learned Fairbanks had made a deal to take over as coach of the University of Colorado Buffaloes following the season. Fairbanks, who like Parcells had a difficult personality but a brilliant football mind, found it increasingly difficult during his tenure to get along with team owner Billy Sullivan. In the end he took the job with Colorado and actually began recruiting for the school without fulfilling his duties to the Pats. Fairbanks was suspended when Sullivan learned of the Colorado deal, and although he was brought back for the first round of the playoffs, his team, which some believed was bound for the Super Bowl, never recovered and was bounced by the Houston Oilers in its first postseason game.

Kraft, too, considered ending the Parcells era early. He later told *The Boston Globe*'s Will McDonough that he considered firing the Tuna following the draft.

Parcells, for his part, decided to stick it out one more season. He resolved privately to have as little as possible to do with Kraft during his final campaign with the Pats. Parcells's refusal to deal with Kraft eventually would force Bill Belichick—who had joined Parcells's coaching staff just that year and who struck up a quick friendship with the owner—into the role of go-between.

Under such strain, the Parcells-Patriots connection might have ended more quickly than the coach anticipated had the season not gone as well as it did. With positive results to rally around, Kraft, the Patriots, and the Tuna were able to keep things together through the regular season, however clumsily and begrudgingly.

Then January rolled around and rumors began to surface that Parcells was planning an exit from New England after the team's last game, and he was likely headed to another team. Reports regarding the contract implications of such a move began to surface with the consensus opinion being that Parcells could leave the Patriots at will, but he couldn't move on to another team without the Pats receiving some kind of compensation since New England owned the coach's rights through the 1997 season.

A week before the Super Bowl, McDonough reported that Parcells would, in fact, be quitting after the game. Parcells denied the veracity of the report, but the troubled relationship between coach and team was too well established, as was McDonough's reputation as a journalist, for the national media to ignore the story. And so began a week in which team members and the coach seemed to spend more time addressing questions of the impending departure than preparing for the game.

The distraction by itself might have been enough to erase the Patriots' already slim chances of upsetting the Packers. But that wasn't the whole of it. Parcells's attention was focused not on the game or the goings on in Super Bowl host city New Orleans, but on finalizing arrangements to jump over to the Jets.

In his 2004 book *Patriot Reign*, journalist Michael Holley reported that the Patriots had phone records from the New Orleans Marriott showing numerous calls from Parcells to Jets headquarters in the week before the game. Holley also quoted Belichick commenting on the difficulties that arose from Parcells's courtship of a new job during Super Bowl week.

Belichick told Holley he found his then-boss's actions "totally inappropriate" given the timing. "How many chances do you get to play for the Super Bowl?" Belichick posed to Holley. "Tell them to get back to you in a couple days."

It's a point worthy of consideration. If Parcells wanted to make a move, why not wait until after the game? What team that wanted him wouldn't have been willing to hold on?

But the Tuna was angry. He wanted out more than he wanted to do right by the players who looked to him for leadership, the team with which he was under contract, and the fans who had invested their faith in him and their ticket dollars in the team. So that's how he played it.

After the game, Parcells declined to travel back to Massachusetts with the team. He'd been done coaching the Patriots for weeks and now it was as good as official.

In a matter of weeks Parcells was in place as coach of the Jets. And the Patriots were on their way to three difficult seasons.

STEPPING IN IT: SPYGATE

When it comes right down to it, the single worst thing about Spygate is that it presented Patriots haters with a tool—or more accurately, a weapon—that they can use forever in their attempts to downplay the accomplishments of the 2007 Patriots and the Belichick-Brady–era New England dynasty in its entirety.

Yes, Spygate resulted in the Patriots losing one of their first-round picks in the 2008 NFL draft. No one will ever know for certain how much that hurt the team, though one can imagine what an organization that drafts as well as New England might have done with the pick. And yes, the team lost $250,000 and Bill Belichick $500,000 in fines as a result of the incident in which a

INSTANT KARMA: 1–15

When the Lisa Olson incident took place, the Patriots were 1–1 on the season, having just topped the division rival Indianapolis Colts 16–14. Fifteen weeks later a 13–10 loss to the New York Giants dropped New England's record to a franchise worst 1–15. With players and coaches distracted by the Olson investigation and an array of other off-field troubles (wide receivers Hart Lee Dykes and Irving Fryar were caught up in legal entanglements), the team became the laughing stock of the league, ranking near the bottom in every statistical category. "The way things are going, they would be no better than even money in an intrasquad scrimmage," *Globe* columnist Bob Ryan wrote of the team. "Each week we ask, 'How can things get worse?' and each week they do."

Pats employee was stopped while videotaping New York Jets defensive coaches' signals from an unapproved location on the sideline in Giants Stadium. But absorbing a $250,000 hit is scarcely a hardship for an NFL franchise. And the mere fact that Belichick is the kind of person who can lose $500,000 without instantly dropping into a coma says all that needs saying about the coach's finances.

The reality, though, is that no matter how much any of the penalties suffered as a result of the illegal videotaping incident may sting, that sensation will fade over time. The team and the coach will make their money back. The lost player's absence will be made manifest only if the team somehow manages to collapse in the 2008 season—an unlikely scenario to say the least—and perhaps not even then. (Though the player drafted in the spot where New England should have picked undoubtedly will always be referenced as the one who might have been a Patriot.) And the loss of that draft pick was mitigated by the fact that it was only one of two first-rounders held by the New England in the '08 draft. And the lower of the pair at that. The pick that was taken away worked out to be the 31st overall. The one the Patriots kept, which they'd acquired in a trade from the San Francisco 49ers during the 2007 draft, landed at seventh overall.

But the haters—whether they're the typical repugnant Internet trolls, loudmouthed sports radio callers, boorish barstool sages, or the purportedly respectable likes of *New York Post* sports editors (who pandered to their Jets fan readers by slapping an asterisk with the words "caught cheating" attached to it onto the Patriots' line in their 2007 NFL standings)—are unlikely ever to go away. As John Madden noted toward the end of the season, a team as good as the Patriots will always manage to draw jealous and fearful detractors. And those Pats detractors will always believe they can diminish the team's accomplishments by referencing Spygate and insisting the Patriots cheated.

And the fact that they're dead wrong won't slow them down one bit.

The simple truth is that those who label the Patriots cheaters as a result of Spygate are trading in willful inaccuracy. The Patriots weren't found guilty of cheating. They weren't penalized for cheating. Nor were they ever actually accused of cheating—at least not by any credible source.

What the Patriots were accused of doing by the Jets on the opening day of the 2007 season, and what the NFL found them guilty of doing and punished them for, was taping from a forbidden location, the sideline.

NOT A MOMENT TOO SOON: THE END OF THE KIAM ERA

It's unlikely that anyone with any common sense or class would ever suggest there was a silver lining to the events surrounding Lisa Olson (or frankly, to the Patriots' 1990 season). But it remains a fact that the incident and Victor Kiam's handling of it likely accelerated Kiam's departure from the Patriots. Kiam, who never should have been accepted by the NFL as a team owner, effectively wore out his welcome by besmirching the reputation of his team and the league during the Olson debacle. Two years later Kiam was gone, and the team was on its way into the hands of Robert Kraft.

When Patriots video assistant Matthew Estrella was stopped from taping Jets coaches some seven minutes into the first quarter of that game, his camera and tape seized and packed off to the league, the only rule he had violated was a rule forbidding such taping from on the field. Had Estrella been engaged in the same activity—capturing defensive coaches' hand signals along with footage of the scoreboard clock (so that the signals could later be paired with plays and, with luck and a lot of work, deciphered)—from an approved location like the coaches' booth above the field, there would have been no issue.

The Patriots gained no strategic advantage in that opening game from Estrella's taping. Had the tape been finished and not seized, the Pats might have gained the ability to predict some Jets defensive plays in the teams' second meeting of the season. But only with luck. The Jets, like most teams, use multiple hand signals coming from different sources to send in plays to their defense, all in order to thwart the universal practice of signal stealing. And even then the Pats would have gained no more strategic advantage over the Jets than they would have by taping from inside the coaches' booth.

The only thing gained by taping from the sideline rather than the booth was a better angle, a closer look at the hand signals being recorded. Of course, that clearly was enough to lead the Patriots to violate a rule that had been emphasized in a memo from the league office in the off-season.

It also had been enough to motivate the Pats to shut down a Jets staffer taping Patriots signals from an unapproved location during a playoff game only eight months earlier. (New England chose not to involve the league in the matter, but Jets officials, including head coach Eric Mangini, have confirmed that the incident took place.)

And that likely speaks to what truly provided the Jets' impetus for touching off Spygate to begin with. It would appear the scandal had more to do with the ongoing feud between the two teams and, more to the point, between Belichick and his former assistant and protégé Mangini, than it ever did with any real concern on the part of the Jets about rules violations or the

GET OFF YOUR HIGH HORSE

In the week leading up to Super Bowl XLII, the former players and coaches from Fox TV's studio show were asked if they believed Spygate tainted the Patriots' incredible season.

"Having coached for nearly 40 years. I can sit and talk for days about all these types of stories and all the things that coaches have done," Jimmy Johnson said.

Howie Long, who's never been accused of loving the Pats, added, "Do you actually believe the New England Patriots were the only team in football filming other teams' sidelines? I think it's a white elephant in the room that no one wants to talk about. ... If you're offended, then be offended by everyone else."

possibility of the Patriots gaining some kind of upper hand in a game to be played later.

There has been no shortage of bad blood between New England and New York since 1997 when Bill Parcells abandoned the Patriots to assume head coaching duties with the Jets—and a year later persuaded standout running back Curtis Martin to join him in East Rutherford. Tensions grew when Belichick fled New Jersey for New England in 2000. And the matter became personal in 2006 when Mangini walked away from the job of Patriots defensive coordinator for the Jets head coaching position.

Belichick, who gave Mangini his start in professional football and brought him along as an assistant in Cleveland, New York, and New England before elevating him to defensive coordinator in 2005, reportedly attempted to talk Mangini out of moving to the hated rival and was rebuffed. The coaches' relationship has been so clearly hostile since then that cameras line up at the end of Pats-Jets games to record their famously cold handshakes.

So the Patriots had stopped the Jets from videotaping in Foxborough during the playoffs. That meant the Jets had to return the favor. They simply didn't stop there. Probably taking note of the league's reminder that such taping is not allowed, they brought the NFL into the matter.

As acts of one-upmanship go, the move was a stunning success.

Not only were the Patriots stopped from taping the Jets' signals, they were eventually forced by the league to give up every tape in their possession. (The league reminded the 31 other teams that taping was not allowed and ordered them to destroy any tapes.) And although the league determined the Patriots had gained no strategic advantage by taping signals, they levied stiff penalties on the team for the rule violation.

The league had little choice but to whack the Patriots hard given the rush of media coverage of Spygate—touched off, interestingly enough, when someone from the Jets tipped off the New York press to the tape seizure.

In the off-season, commissioner Roger Goodell had leveled significant sanctions against players as a result of conduct detrimental to the league's image. He suspended Adam "Pacman" Jones and quarterback Michael Vick each for a full season and defensive tackle Tank Johnson for eight games, all for off-the-field activities. Spygate put a team in Goodell's crosshairs for the first time. A highly successful team at that. And for violating a rule Goodell had taken pains to emphasize. The commissioner had little choice but to come down hard on the Patriots for what was widely perceived as a significant infraction—even if it really was not.

All of that might have been enough, perhaps more than enough, to satisfy the Jets. But they got more: the *Post's* asterisk, the tagging of Belichick as Belicheat, the assertion by assorted players and experts with axes to grind (among them retired Miami Dolphins coach Don Shula, who later recanted) that the Patriots' season had been tainted and the ability, in perpetuity, of Jets fans and other assorted Patriots haters to assert that nothing the Pats have achieved really counts.

They're wrong. But the Patriots and their fans will always have to deal with them. In some ways, it doesn't get any uglier than that.

TWO VICIOUS HITS, ONE FREAK ACCIDENT

THE WORST INJURY IN PATRIOTS HISTORY: DARRYL STINGLEY

There comes a moment once every three or four seasons when football fans are reminded—suddenly, painfully, horribly—of what a savage sport football can be.

Ninety percent of the time, it begins with nothing more than two players doing their jobs. An offensive player doing everything he can to advance the ball. A defender going all out to stop him. A collision. Brutal. But in nearly every important way not unlike the other brutal collisions that take place on fields across the country every Sunday during the fall and early winter.

Then one of the players involved—usually the one taking the hit rather than the one administering it—fails to get up. And it becomes clear that he hasn't simply had the wind knocked out of him. And that what's happened isn't merely game ending or season ending, but career ending.

Sometimes the replay shows precisely what happened. Joe Theismann's leg snaps like dry kindling under the weight and power of Lawrence Taylor. Sometimes it's not so clear. Buffalo Bills tight end Kevin Everett, while pitching in on special teams, goes down after a collision with Denver Broncos kick returner Domenik Hixon with what will later be revealed as a spinal injury. Either way, by the time you see the injured player being carried off the field, you know it's the last time you'll ever see him in pads and a uniform.

It's the worst part of the game.

Almost no one who wasn't present in Oakland, California, on August 12, 1978, saw Darryl Stingley being carried off the field. It was the preseason. It was the '70s, long before cable TV and ravenous fans turned every minor occurrence in the NFL into a media event. It was the middle of summer, when people had better things to do than follow exhibition football games.

By the end of the day, however, most football fans—and especially those in New England—not only had heard about Stingley's injury, but also had seen the hit that caused it on the evening news. Many have seen it more than a few times since. And every time it's as brutal and horrific—and as stunningly ordinary—as the last.

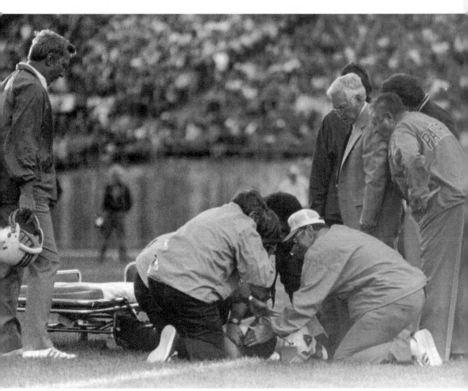

Patriots wide receiver Darryl Stingley lies motionless on the field after taking a brutal hit from the Raiders' Jack Tatum at Oakland Coliseum on August 12, 1978.

ADDING INSULT TO INJURY

It would be one thing if Jack Tatum had simply failed to appreciate the inhumanity of his post-injury attitude toward Darryl Stingley. But that, apparently, wasn't enough for the Assassin. Apparently unsatisfied with the mere fact that he'd built a good part of his reputation as an NFL badass on the misery he inflicted on Stingley, Tatum eventually would try to exploit the crippled ex-wideout for personal gain. Tatum, who never visited Stingley in the hospital and who steadfastly refused to express any remorse for what had happened, did approach the late wide receiver on occasion to try to arrange an on-air discussion. Tatum did that whenever he had a book to promote. Stingley always declined.

Stingley, the wide receiver, extends, putting in the extra effort that was his stock in trade in an attempt to pull down a pass from quarterback Steve Grogan that had sailed a bit too high. Doing his job. Then Oakland Raiders safety Jack Tatum comes flying in, full of the fury he was famous for, and pulverizes Stingley. Tatum's forearm and helmet crash into Stingley's helmet, hammering the defenseless receiver to the ground. Stingley collapses to the field. And he never makes it back to his feet. Never.

Stingley would never walk, nor even use his arms in any real way, after that hit. The two broken vertebrae he suffered in that preseason game left Stingley a quadriplegic. The injury also led to his early death on April 5, 2007, at the age of 55.

There remains, even 30 years later with Stingley in the ground and Tatum reportedly losing a long battle with diabetes, division over the hit that cost Stingley almost everything.

There are those who believe the hit was unnecessarily vicious, dirty, and uncalled for. It was a preseason game with nothing meaningful on the line, they argue. Tatum should have recognized that Stingley had no hope of catching the pass and pulled up.

Grogan is one of those. He has maintained over the years that the hit was late and that Tatum had to know the play was effectively over before he ever reached Stingley. Grogan also hasn't been shy about criticizing Tatum for the way he acted immediately after the hit and in all the years thereafter.

Tatum never made any attempt to show remorse for what had happened or concern for the man he'd crippled. While his coach, John Madden, and teammates spent time with Stingley in the hospital, Tatum stayed away, insisting he had nothing to say to the injured player. And not only did Tatum's position on the matter never soften, he made something of a post-football career out of sneering at Stingley.

Tatum, who always embraced his nickname, "Assassin," has written three books about his experiences in the NFL, *They Call Me Assassin, They Still Call Me Assassin,* and *Final Confessions of NFL Assassin.* In each book Tatum celebrates his crushing playing style, taking pride in the fact that the hits he administered frequently seemed designed not to stop offensive players but to injure them. In his last book Tatum criticized defensive players who came along after his time for not being savage enough, claiming that if he'd played the way current players do "Darryl Stingley wouldn't be confined to a wheelchair."

And that approach to the incident has always placed Tatum well outside the range of normal, understandable human behavior. Even the hardest hitters in the game have typically expressed horror when their play has resulted in serious injury. Taylor, for instance, frantically called for medical attention for Theismann after his famous hit, broke down on the field, and has said he has never been able to watch the play.

That Tatum not only insists he did nothing wrong in his hit on Stingley, but also actually boasts of the results, certainly colors the way Grogan and other critics perceive the events.

"It was Jack Tatum that was the real problem, when he was bragging about the fact that he had done what he'd done to Darryl," Grogan said in an interview on Boston sports radio station WEEI the day Stingley died. "That was what was hard to take."

Looking at the hit, it's hard not to conclude that Tatum's personality was ultimately more problematic than his play.

The blow Tatum delivered to Stingley was without question intended to punish. Tatum clearly wanted to make sure Stingley would forever be looking over his shoulder any time the two men found themselves on the same field.

Tatum had to know that was the only way to slow a receiver like Stingley, a possession guy whose greatest quality was that he put every bit of himself into every play whether he was throwing a block (not an unusual role for a receiver in Chuck Fairbanks and Ron Erhardt's run-oriented offenses) or making tough catches while operating against tight coverage underneath. Stingley wasn't always the most gifted receiver on a field (though sometimes he was), but he was usually the hardest working. And the toughest. If you didn't get into his head, he posed a continuous threat.

But Tatum's hit was legal at the time. (It was partially as a result of that play that rules were later put in place to protect defenseless receivers. And it's those rules, in combination with rules protecting quarterbacks, that have made the passing game a big part of professional football.) It may have been ill-advised. It

LOSING A JOB TO AN INJURY

When Drew Bledsoe was cleared to play in week 11 of the 2001 season, many fans and experts believed he should and would be given his job back. Never mind that Tom Brady had started to come on and was leading the Pats to success and showing a degree of smarts and a knack for the game that surpassed Bledsoe's, there was considered to be an unwritten rule in the NFL that quarterbacks didn't lose their jobs as a result of injury. Bill Belichick, however, wasn't interested in unwritten rules. He stuck with the guy with a knack for his system and an amazing grasp of football strategy. Five months later, the Pats were world champions and Bledsoe was on his way to Buffalo. No one has asked Belichick about unwritten rules since.

may have been unnecessary. But it was within the rules. And Tatum was simply playing the way he always played—whatever anyone might think of that.

That doesn't change anything, of course. It doesn't give Stingley his legs, or his life, back. It doesn't change the fact that the Patriots lost a player who was a leader on the field and off, a player who led the team in receptions the previous season and who might have had another half dozen good to great years in him.

It doesn't make Tatum any less wrong for the way he handled himself after that day, either. The only thing that ever could have redeemed Tatum would have been an apology. And now, as of April 5, 2007, the day Stingley died, it will always be too late for that.

THE HIT THAT CHANGED EVERYTHING: DREW BLEDSOE GOES DOWN

The most important thing to note about the hit Mo Lewis put on Drew Bledsoe on September 23, 2001, is that no one lost a career or, more importantly, the use of his legs and arms as a result of it. In at least that regard, Lewis's sideline strike on the Patriots' star quarterback was different from the Jack Tatum hit that had crippled Darryl Stingley 23 years earlier.

But the hit on Bledsoe wasn't entirely unlike the hit on Stingley. It did effectively end Bledsoe's career as a Patriot. Though the quarterback would see action in relief of Tom Brady during a playoff game that season, he would never again start for the Pats. The hit did result in a horrific injury. And it was, while legal, a good bit more of a blow than the situation called for. The hit appeared for all the world as if it were intended to cause injury. At the very least it left the impression that Lewis, a linebacker for the New York Jets, cared much more about making sure Bledsoe never forgot him than he did about the potential consequences of his actions. It was a cheap shot.

The hit came at the end of a play during a losing effort. It was the second game of the season (the first after a week in which all NFL play was suspended following the September 11 attacks), and the Patriots were trailing 10–3 late in the fourth quarter. Bledsoe,

Patriots quarterback Drew Bledsoe, sporting a beard, stretches during a practice on January 10, 2002.

who had performed adequately in spite of the absence of a running game in a loss in Cincinnati two weeks earlier, was struggling outright this time around. He was 18 for 28 passing on the day and had thrown two interceptions.

On third-and-10 from the Patriots 19 with a pass rush coming on, Bledsoe rolled out of the pocket and scrambled for eight yards before giving up on making the first-down marker and turning for the sideline. Nearly everyone involved, recognizing the play was over, reined it in. Everyone, that is, except Lewis. The linebacker slammed full force into Bledsoe, knocking the ball out of the quarterback's hand and sending his target flying over the sideline. Bledsoe crashed to the ground and lay there for a minute before rising back to his feet. He appeared to shake off the cobwebs and reentered the game after the Jets went three and out.

But it quickly became apparent that something was wrong. Bill Belichick pulled Bledsoe and sent in Brady for the final minutes of the game. Bledsoe was sent to Massachusetts General Hospital, where it was discovered he'd been bleeding internally as a result of a partially torn artery and a sheared blood vessel. Blood was drained from Bledsoe's chest, but the quarterback remained hospitalized for much of the week. When he was released, he was ordered to refrain from any strenuous activity for at least two weeks. Ultimately it would be nine weeks before he was finally cleared to play again.

When the news broke in the wake of the Jets game that Bledsoe would be unable to play indefinitely, the Patriots' season appeared lost. And there was good reason for believing that.

Setting aside the truly horrific—think Darryl Stingley or Mike Utley injuries—you can break pro football injuries down like this: there are the injuries that take out a star quarterback, and then there are all the others.

No single player in the game, particularly in the pass-oriented style of play that currently dominates the NFL, is half as important to the success of his team as the man taking the snaps and making the throws.

This has never been more true than in the salary-cap era. The introduction of the cap, along with free agency, in 1994 didn't

NOT CONTENT TO SIT

Darryl Stingley never let his injury define who he was. Confined to a wheelchair and able to live well off what he'd earned as a player and the substantial injury settlement he received from the Patriots, Stingley could easily have retreated into his Chicago home and left the world behind. He didn't. Instead, he created a nonprofit foundation through which he worked to help troubled inner-city kids turn their lives around and find hope. Stingley, it turned out, was 10 times the man Jack Tatum was, even after Tatum did his best to take everything away from him.

make quarterbacks any less expensive. And that's made the best passers ever more vital to their teams.

In a given year a good starting QB might account for 10 to 12 percent of a team's total allotment under the cap. That's 12 percent of total salary devoted to one person on a 53-man roster. It leaves 88 percent of cap space to spread out among 98 percent of the players on a team—and less than 88 percent if the team has to account for dead money (cap space chewed up by past years' bonuses paid to players no longer on the roster) or is smart enough to hold money aside to bring in new players as a season wears on.

Add to that the attrition rate that's part of managing an NFL team. No team makes it through an entire season without losing an offensive or defensive lineman, defensive back, receiver, or running back for at least a handful of games. More often than not, teams lose starters at more than one position for some stretch. That makes depth at most positions essential to any team that hopes to mount a successful campaign.

So even if it were possible to maintain two proven standout quarterbacks on a roster—keeping in mind that there rarely are 32 quarterbacks in the league who are clearly qualified to *start* games, let alone star in them (nor even the 31 who would have been needed in 2001)—the financial burden would leave a team unable to maintain real depth anywhere else. That would constitute a disaster waiting to happen.

Six months before Drew Bledsoe was injured, he signed a 10-year, $103 million deal. Bledsoe's cap charge for the 2001 season was just more than $8 million, a major chunk of that season's $67 million cap. But there was good reason for that. Bledsoe was the franchise, the first overall draft choice who had led the Patriots to the Super Bowl five seasons earlier and who was, at the time, one of the most popular players ever to wear a Patriots uniform.

The guy behind Bledsoe on the depth chart, by contrast, was a second-year player out of Michigan who'd been selected in the sixth round (199th overall), who was making all of $300,000 for the season, and who 99 percent of Patriots fans had heard of in passing if at all.

So the idea that Brady would have to lead the team, potentially through most of the season, was more than scary; it was downright depressing. The Pats had struggled mightily since Bill Parcells had abandoned them after the 1996 season. And two games into their second year under their second head coach since Parcells's departure, it appeared Mo Lewis had stolen any hope of success.

That, of course, turned out to be precisely the opposite of what would happen. Bledsoe never started again for the Patriots not because he couldn't, but because it worked out that his $300,000-a-year backup was the better quarterback.

Years later, with Brady having led the team to three Super Bowl championships and a perfect regular season, piling up NFL records on the way, it's easy to joke about the hit that took Bledsoe out of the picture (particularly in light of Bledsoe's recovery and his years spent as a starter in Buffalo and Dallas). It's interesting to imagine how the recent history of the team and the league might have been different had Lewis pulled up that day. And it's not uncommon to hear Patriots fans talk about Lewis as the man who saved the Pats. (Unlike Tatum, Lewis no doubt *would* do things differently if given another chance—though it would likely be for all the wrong reasons.)

But it's important, somehow, to remember that things didn't feel that way at all on September 23, 2001. There wasn't a Pats fan in New England who would have congratulated Lewis on his hard hit that day.

FLAG FOOTBALL? ROBERT EDWARDS

Chances are, Robert Edwards was never going to be Curtis Martin. Players as good as Martin just don't come along all that often.

But Edwards might have turned out to be a damned good tailback.

Might have. If he hadn't suffered what has to count as the worst flag football injury in NFL history.

Edwards was a good prospect coming out of the University of Georgia in 1998, and the Pats were in need of a starting running back.

Bill Parcells had used his inside knowledge of New England's salary cap situation to craft an offer to Martin, a restricted free agent, that the Patriots couldn't hope to match. It was a brilliant move by the Tuna. Martin was the NFL Offensive Rookie of the Year under Parcells in 1995, rushing for 1,487 yards and

WHAT ELSE COULD HE DO?

Andy Katzenmoyer looked like he might turn out to be one of the greats when the Patriots took him with one of their two first-round picks in the 1999 draft (28th overall). Katzenmoyer was a tough, physical middle linebacker who had won the Butkus Award in his junior year at Ohio State. He had a solid rookie season, recording 107 tackles and three and a half sacks. He also picked off a Dan Marino pass and returned it 57 yards for a touchdown. In 2000, however, he suffered a neck injury that required surgery. A year later he walked out of training camp, saying he had a feeling in his neck that concerned him. Some Pats fans have never forgiven Katzenmoyer. But, really, what choice did he have?

14 touchdowns. He'd been to two Pro Bowls in three seasons. He was headed for the Hall of Fame and Parcells knew it. In one relatively easy stroke, Parcells simultaneously improved his team and hurt a division rival.

The deal cost the Jets picks in the first and third rounds of the '98 draft, but Martin was undoubtedly worth the price.

The Patriots had little choice but to try to use one of their first-round picks to replace their leading rusher. They looked into moving up in the draft but couldn't make a deal. So they sat tight at 18th overall and were happy when Edwards fell to them.

Edwards had shown great breakaway speed at Georgia. He was a straight-ahead runner who could bolt through defenses for big gains and was also powerful enough to use in short yardage situations.

The Pats appeared to have received good value out of their pick during Edwards' rookie season. Edwards ran for 1,115 yards and nine touchdowns, and picked up an additional 331 yards and three TDs on 35 receptions. His rookie year wasn't at the level of Martin's, but his overall production was better than Martin's had been in 1997.

There was reason to feel good about what Edwards could bring to the team, particularly if the rest of the offense could improve heading into 1999. (Drew Bledsoe had a subpar season in '98, and the team struggled to a 9–7 finish.) Edwards hadn't qualified for the Pro Bowl, but he had been invited to take part in the rookie four-on-four flag football tournament held on Waikiki Beach the Friday before the All-Star game.

That invitation ultimately cost Edwards his career in the NFL.

In the course of the game, Edwards jumped to deflect a pass thrown by Detroit Lions quarterback Charlie Batch. Oakland Raiders cornerback Charles Woodson, Edwards' teammate in the flag game, went after the same pass. And when the two players came down, Woodson landed on Edwards's left leg.

Edwards lay in the sand for several minutes waiting for medical help. He was carried off the field and taken to the hospital where doctors discovered that Edwards's knee had been severely dislocated and that the injury had damaged an artery.

WE HART LEE KNEW HIM

Off the field Hart Lee Dykes was probably a bit more like his teammate Irving Fryar than anyone was really comfortable with. Dykes was with Fryar when they got into a bar fight, in which Dykes suffered an eye injury that cost him six games in the 1990 season. On the field Dykes showed lots of potential, though most of it went unrealized. Dykes was tall and fast and might have evolved into a fine receiver if he had learned to elude tacklers. But Dykes never had a chance. The 16th overall pick in the 1989 draft suffered a fractured right kneecap during a preseason game in 1991. He attempted a comeback two years later, but blew out his left knee in training camp.

They operated and narrowly avoided having to amputate Edwards's lower leg.

Within a day it had been reported that Edwards would be lost at least for the 1999 season and that he likely would never play another down.

And while those reports ultimately proved inaccurate—Edwards, after undergoing extensive rehab on the knee, attempted a comeback with the Miami Dolphins in 2002 and has since had three successful seasons in the Canadian Football League—the hope Edwards represented for the Patriots was lost.

It would be 2001 before another Patriots running back would top 1,000 yards in a season.

IN THE CLUTCH

BLIZZARD CONDITIONS: ADAM VINATIERI AND THE GREATEST KICK EVER MADE

There's only one greatest feeling you can experience as a professional football fan: the one you feel watching your team win a Super Bowl.

But second best isn't quite as far off as someone who hasn't felt both might imagine. And it doesn't come from seeing your team win a conference championship. Or from watching them vanquish a hated opponent.

The second-finest feeling a fan can have comes from seeing your team do something that's never been done before and will almost certainly never be done again. It's about knowing, even as you watch events unfold, that you're not just seeing team history but league history in the making.

It's being there as Alan Ameche lunges across the goal line to secure the Baltimore Colts' overtime victory in the 1958 NFL Championship. It's watching Franco Harris scoop up the Immaculate Reception or seeing John Elway engineer the Drive.

If you're a Patriots fan, you've had more than your fair share of opportunities to experience that sensation in the recent past. Maybe you picked up the vibe while watching Tom Brady and Randy Moss break single-season records for touchdown passes (50) and touchdown receptions (23) on the same play in the final week of the 2007 season. Or standing witness as Adam Vinatieri's 41-yarder at the end of Super Bowl XXXVIII made him the only kicker in league history to nail game-winning field goals in two Super Bowls.

If you've been around for the long haul, though, it's unlikely anything will ever compare with watching Vinatieri boot the ball 45 yards through the driving snow to pull the Pats into a tie with the Oakland Raiders in the 2001 AFC divisional playoffs.

That moment stands apart from every other instance of Patriots history in two important ways.

The biggest at the time, though its importance has been dulled some as a result of subsequent events, was that it marked the first time the Pats had made an enduring mark in the books in a way that reflected positively on the team. New England wasn't on the losing end of a blowout of epic proportions this time. The team hadn't beaten the Miami Dolphins 3–0 with help from a snowplow or lost 6–0 to the New York Jets in the middle of a monsoon. And this surely wasn't the Stupor Bowl, the 1981 game that pitted the 2–13 Patriots against the 1–14 Baltimore Colts and marked the worst closing week matchup in NFL history. (The game was such a thoroughly upside-down affair that the loser was the winner—or at least it seemed that way at the time. By falling to the Colts, the Pats captured the first overall pick in the 1982 draft, which they promptly wasted on defensive end Kenneth Sims.)

But there was, and still is, another way in which that moment stood apart from every other instance of the Pats making league history. It's that no one, but no one, ever saw it coming.

More than that, most fans who were watching weren't entirely sure they could trust their eyes even as they saw the ball clear the crossbar.

That's what makes the kick so unforgettable. Vinatieri never should have made it. In fact, had the situation not been desperate, there's little doubt the attempt would never have been made.

Forget that Vinatieri had yet to establish himself as the NFL's greatest clutch kicker on January 19, 2002. It wouldn't have mattered that evening if it were known he would eventually set records for making game-winning kicks. It wouldn't have mattered if he'd had a perfect record through his six-year

NFL career up to that point (which, of course, he didn't). The fact is that no one could have been expected to make that kick in those conditions.

The snow had started falling early that afternoon. Falling heavy. There were already a few inches on the ground by game

Adam Vinatieri kicks a 45-yard field goal to tie the game with 27 seconds left in the fourth quarter against the Oakland Raiders in their AFC Divisional Playoff game in Foxborough, Massachusetts, on January 19, 2002.

time, and the snow never let up through the late afternoon and early evening. It kept coming hard and strong. And it came with the usual freezing, bitter wind whipping the falling flakes around to the point where everything and everyone was framed in white. You couldn't see through the snow well enough to drive safely. Hell, you could hardly see through it well enough to walk safely.

The weather knocked both teams out of their offenses. As the fourth quarter drew toward a close, the Patriots and Raiders, teams that had averaged 23 and 25 points per game during the season, had managed just 23 points between them. The Raiders led 13–10, and there was no reason to expect, as the Patriots started a final drive just before the two-minute warning, that they'd be able to move downfield quickly enough to win or tie the game.

Even after an apparent Tom Brady fumble that would have sealed victory for the Raiders was overturned on review (referee Walt Coleman determined that Brady had been in the process of completing a throwing motion when the ball came out of his hand, which meant the play was an incomplete pass, not a fumble), things seemed mostly bleak for the Pats. Brady was able to move the team to the Raiders' 29-yard line, but the offense stalled there. Three plays later the Pats had advanced the ball a total of one yard. It was fourth-and-nine with 32 seconds remaining on the clock. A field goal was a long shot to say the least, but nothing else was working. A kick had to be worth a try.

With no timeouts remaining the Patriots had all they could do to get the offense off the field and the field-goal unit onto it. There was no time for holder Ken Walter to clear a spot to place the ball, meaning Walter would have to place the ball on the approximately four inches of packed snow that covered the field. And Vinatieri would have do his best to plant and kick from atop the glacier through a pair of uprights barely visible through the furious whiteout.

Everyone involved exhibited uncanny poise in the horrid conditions, from the offensive linemen who never flinched, to long

THE SNOWPLOW GAME

The NFL has a rule barring the use of snowplows on the field during a game. But it didn't on December 12, 1982. So when the Pats got close to the Miami Dolphins' end zone late in the fourth quarter of a 0–0 game—played on a Schaefer Stadium surface more suited to curling than football—coach Ron Meyer called for a plow. And Mark Henderson obliged. A prison inmate on work release with the stadium ground crew, Henderson cleared a spot on the field for kicker John Smith, whose 33-yard boot made the difference in a 3–0 Pats victory. Pats fans roared. Miami coach Don Shula freaked. And when the season ended, the NFL rules committee had one easy order of business.

snapper Lonie Paxton, who hit Walter with the perfection he's exhibited throughout his eight-year career, to Walter who took the snap and placed the ball with more precision under impossible circumstances than some holders (read: Tony Romo) could in perfect conditions.

And while no one will ever argue that the kick Vinatieri made was the prettiest or the surest of his career, the kicker did precisely what he needed to do.

The kick came out low, as it typically will in a long field goal attempt, but instead of rising steadily as it moved toward the goal post, it seemed to get up just overhead and then stick there. The ball clearly had enough leg on it. And almost miraculously it appeared to be en route to somewhere between the uprights. But as it shot toward the goal post, there remained the question of whether it would be high enough to pass over the crossbar. It was, if only just.

The kick hadn't won the game. The field goal that would do that wouldn't come until eight and a half minutes into overtime. And it would come from a paltry 23 yards out.

But that didn't matter. What did matter was that the Patriots, who only minutes earlier appeared to be headed for yet another in a long series of postseason disappointments, had for once made the most of their opportunities. Having been spared certain doom deus ex machina style by the replay booth, they had managed to keep the drama moving forward. What doubt could there be, then, that the team would find a way to manufacture a happy ending in the extra period?

Even when they did, though, even as the team celebrated, hugging on the sideline, dancing on the field, Paxton making snow angels in the end zone, and as fans filed out of the old stadium for the last time into the still-falling snow or stared at each other gape-jawed across living rooms and bars, the question that lingered, and that lingers still, wasn't, "Can you believe they did it?" It was, "Can you believe that kick?"

SUPER CLUTCH: VINATIERI COMES THROUGH IN THE BIGGEST MOMENT IMAGINABLE—TWICE

Consider this: only nine times in the 42-year history of the Super Bowl has professional football's championship been decided by the game's last meaningful play.

Despite the fact that the game ostensibly pairs the two best teams in football, the Super Bowl more often than not has proven a lopsided affair.

More than that, in five of the nine instances in which the game has come down to its last play, the winning play has been a defensive stop. Think St. Louis linebacker Mike Jones' goal-line tackle of Tennessee wide receiver Kevin Dyson as time expired in Super Bowl XXXIV. Or Rodney Harrison's pickoff of Philadelphia quarterback Donovan McNabb to seal the Patriots' victory in Super Bowl XXXIX.

The only two game-changing touchdowns ever scored truly late in the Super Bowl came with 34 and 35 seconds remaining on the clock. In Super Bowl XXIII, Joe Montana found John Taylor in the end zone to put San Francisco up 20–16 over Cincinnati with 34 seconds remaining. And as New England fans know all too well, Eli Manning won Super Bowl XLII with a strike to Plaxico

Burress that left just 35 seconds for the Patriots to attempt a miracle comeback. In each of those games, however, the winning team's defense had to finish the game by breaking up desperation pass attempts.

The Super Bowl has come down to a field-goal attempt in the closing seconds on four occasions. In Super Bowl V, Jim O'Brien hit from 32 yards out with five seconds remaining to lift the Baltimore Colts over the Dallas Cowboys. Twenty years later Buffalo kicker Scott Norwood missed on a 47-yard try at the very end of regulation, preserving the New York Giants' one-point victory in Super Bowl XXV.

The Super Bowl's two other game-winning kicks were made by Adam Vinatieri. One as time expired in Super Bowl XXXVI, the other with four seconds left to play in Super Bowl XXXVIII.

So not only is Vinatieri the only player ever to account for the winning points in two Super Bowls, he also can claim responsibility for two of only three offensive plays ever to have won the game in its closing seconds. That fact alone makes Vinatieri a fairly safe bet for eventual enshrinement in the Pro Football Hall of Fame. (Players become eligible five years after retirement. And it isn't any kind of a stretch to assume Vinatieri will be elected on his first ballot.) It also at least qualifies him for inclusion in any conversation about the best kickers of all time.

And when talking about the game's greatest clutch kicker, there's little room for discussion. No one has ever had anything approaching Vinatieri's success kicking in pressure situations.

Vinatieri's postseason game winners are only part of an incredible overall picture. During his 12-year career in the NFL—which has included 10 seasons with the Patriots and two with the Indianapolis Colts—Vinatieri has accounted for a go-ahead score in the final minute of a game 20 times. His sole miss in the clutch came in 1999 when he bounced a 32-yard kick off the upright in Kansas City's Arrowhead Stadium. And even then, punter/holder Lee Johnson went out of his way to take the blame.

"I got the ball caught on my thumb, and I couldn't get the laces around," Johnson told reporters after the game. "It was what

I call a three o'clock lace, with the laces on the right side of the ball. And when that happens the kick usually goes wide right."

It's also worth noting that Vinatieri had, at that point in the '99 season, put up the winning points in three of New England's four victories. His go-ahead scores in two of those matches—a week-one win over the Jets in New Jersey and a week-two home victory over the Colts—had come with three minutes and 30 seconds left on the clock.

That's how good Vinatieri was during his time with the Pats. It's why fans and the Boston media alike fretted mightily when Automatic Adam opted to bolt Foxborough for Indianapolis in free agency during the 2006 off-season. And why Vinatieri was embraced robustly by fans of the Colts, who'd been burned by Vinatieri over the years nearly as often as they'd been let down by Mike Vanderjagt.

But setting all of that, as well as Vinatieri's well-earned nickname, aside, nothing is ever really automatic in the NFL, least of all 48-yard field goals in the crushing high-pressure atmosphere of a Super Bowl. So it was anything but a given as the field goal unit lined up in the final seconds of Super Bowl XXXVI that Vinatieri would be able to complete the Pats' upset of the St. Louis Rams.

To that point Vinatieri's only notable moment in a championship game had come in his rookie season when he booted the kickoff Desmond Howard returned 99 yards for the touchdown that secured Super Bowl XXXI for the Green Bay Packers.

He'd been spot-on to that point in the game against the Rams, though, hitting a 37-yarder late in the third quarter that put the Pats up 17–3. And the kick he was being asked to make after a Tom Brady spike at the Rams' 30-yard line stopped the clock with seven seconds remaining wasn't a win-or-lose proposition. A miss would simply have sent the game into overtime.

There was, however, the matter of the rally the Rams had mounted in the final period. And the fact that St. Louis had come into the game a heavy favorite. Even discounting questions of momentum, the Pats were in no position to squander any opportunity to wrap things up, however long the odds.

The kick Vinatieri made in the closing seconds of that game wasn't anything like the one he'd made to beat the Raiders two weeks earlier. You could see it was good coming off his foot.

Of course, unless you were completely unaware of Patriots history, you still held your breath waiting for something awful to happen to the ball. Maybe a bird would swoop down and knock it off course. Maybe it would simply stop dead in midair. Or explode due to some odd natural phenomenon that would be explained later—and again every time the event was recounted with much laughter and bemused shaking of heads over the years. Or, you know, maybe the Pats would be called for a false start and the 10-second runoff would send the game to overtime.

But there was never, not for so much as a second, any doubt but that the kick itself was exactly what it needed to be.

Vinatieri knew it, too.

"Once I kicked it, I knew it was good," he said after the game. "I wasn't nervous."

Vinatieri would have been well within reason to feel nervous two years later when he took the field at the end of Super Bowl XXXVIII with the scored tied at 29.

Vinatieri was 0–2 at that point in the game, having pushed a 31-yard try right on the Pats' first drive of the game and had a 36-yarder blocked in the second quarter. And given that he'd missed two other kicks in that year's Super Bowl venue, Reliant Stadium in Houston, during a week 12 game against the Texans, Vinatieri might easily have concluded he was up against not just the game clock and the Carolina Panthers' rushers but a powerful jinx.

He didn't.

Vinatieri told *Sports Illustrated*'s Don Banks after the game he had just one thing in mind as he set up to try the 41-yard kick for the win.

"It just came down to rhythm, and to win this thing and get the heck out of here," he said.

As with the kick at the end of Super Bowl XXXVI, there was no question once the ball came off Vinatieri's foot that it would do the job. And this time as the ball sailed through the air there was no reason for fans to expect some freak accident. No one was nervous because no one needed to be. The Pats were going to be champions for the second time in three years. And for the second time in three years, Adam Vinatieri would be the guy swinging the score New England's way at the very end.

That kind of performance in football's biggest game is the definition of clutch.

THE DIFFERENCE: TROY BROWN STEPS UP

Troy Brown is a Patriot the way John "Hog" Hannah is a Patriot. The way Steve Grogan and Gino Cappelletti are Patriots. Now and forever. Wherever he goes. Whatever he does. His dues are paid in full. His membership is irrevocable.

That status didn't come as a gift, either. It's not some token of appreciation for 15 years of dedicated service. Brown *earned* the respect and admiration of the Patriots faithful. Just like he earned everything in his career.

His game-saving performance against the Pittsburgh Steelers in the 2001–02 AFC Championship game is just part of the picture. Not an unimportant part, but a part that's been obscured by history, lost in the excitement over the *bigger* events of that postseason—the unbelievable divisional round win over the Oakland Raiders and the incredible Super Bowl victory over the St. Louis Rams.

It shouldn't be.

Forget the obvious: the fact that teams don't earn a trip to the Super Bowl without winning a conference championship and the fact that a win in the divisional round, however exciting, loses meaning quickly if it's the last victory of the season. What matters most about the January 27 game in Pittsburgh was that it was another postseason match no one thought the Pats could win. And if it weren't for Troy Brown, they very likely wouldn't have.

The Pats went into Pittsburgh as nine-point underdogs. They were seeded second in the AFC, having finished the season with a record of 11–5, but the Steelers, who won 13 games during the regular season, were seeded first and were considered hands-down the best team in the conference. The Steelers were a well-balanced team. Their offense finished the season ranked seventh in the league; their defense ranked third. (The Pats ranked sixth in both categories, but had barely survived a home game against a decidedly unbalanced Raiders team—Oakland was all offense—a week earlier.)

It was *supposed* to be Pittsburgh's year.

The only trouble with that was that it *was* Troy Brown's year.

It was the year Brown had been building toward since he joined the Patriots in 1993. And it was achieved by way of the work ethic that had kept Brown, an eighth-round draft choice out of Division 1-AA Marshall University, hanging around for nine years to that point.

A standout punt and kick returner in college, Brown was brought in primarily to serve as a special teamer for the Pats. And through the bulk of his first seven seasons that was most of what he did. He was made a full-time pass catcher in 1997 and proved to be a standout possession receiver, hauling in 41 balls for 607

Wide receiver Troy Brown returns a punt during a game against the Miami Dolphins in Foxborough, Massachusetts, on December 23, 2007.

TOUCHDOWNS, TOO: VINATIERI HITS TROY BROWN

Adam Vinatieri also had one exciting moment during his tenure with the Patriots that had nothing to do with kicking. In a week nine visit to St. Louis during the 2004 season, Vinatieri completed a four-yard touchdown pass to Troy Brown. The TD was scored from a field-goal formation with Brown hidden out on the far left side of the field. The Rams failed to notice Brown, who stepped forward uncovered to the 1-yard line, snagged Vinatieri's perfectly thrown pass, and darted into the end zone. The play put the Pats ahead 26–14 in a game they would win 40–22.

yards and six touchdowns while playing mainly in the slot (with Terry Glenn and Shawn Jefferson lined up wide). But he resumed return duties the following season (while continuing to play receiver), largely at his own insistence. Returning kicks was what helped Brown make it to the pros. It's what had kept him there. And he simply wasn't willing to give it up.

He kept on returning kicks even as he became an ever more important part of the passing game in 2000.

In 2001 Brown became the team's leading receiver. Serving as young Tom Brady's most reliable target, he hauled in 101 catches for 1,199 yards and five TDs, earning a trip to the Pro Bowl in the process. And still, he remained a blue-collar guy at heart. Brown never turned his back on his role as a special teamer, returning 29 punts in 2001, including a career-best two for touchdowns, both in the final four weeks of the season.

Fittingly, though he had an outstanding day as a receiver, it was most noticeably as a special teamer that Brown made his biggest mark in the postseason. And he did it with two spectacular plays precisely when his team most needed the help.

Brown's first big moment in Pittsburgh came relatively early. With four minutes remaining in the first quarter, no points on the board, and the game looking increasingly like it would be a purely defensive struggle, Brown dropped back to return Josh Miller's third punt of the day. Wary of Brown's return abilities, the Steelers had come into the game determined to contain him. They'd had spotty success to that point, giving up 25 yards on Brown's first return but cornering him for no gain on his second.

This time out, with Miller punting from deep inside Steelers territory, the Pittsburgh coverage team was on high alert. They appeared to catch a break as Miller boomed a 64-yard kick that rolled dead at the New England 23-yard line. But officials flagged Steelers wideout Troy Edwards, who was in on coverage, for stepping out of bounds, forcing Miller to punt again, this time from Pittsburgh's 8-yard line.

Brown took the kick at the New England 45 and, as was his wont, barreled straight down the center of Pittsburgh's coverage. He slipped by one defender, then another, leaped over a downed third, then cut loose for the end zone with a few Steelers continuing to give half-hearted pursuit knowing they had no chance of catching him.

Brown's 55-yard carry marked the first time in AFC Championship history that a punt had been returned for a touchdown.

It was a huge moment, one in which everyone watching became aware that contrary to expectations the Patriots absolutely were capable of advancing to the Super Bowl. Its true significance, however, wouldn't become evident until much later.

Brown's real importance to the team started to become clear late in the second quarter when Brady had to leave the game with an ankle injury. Having just hit Brown with a 28-yard strike that moved the Pats into Pittsburgh territory for just the second time in the game, Brady was hit from behind by Steelers safety Lee Flowers. He left the field gimpy and was replaced by Drew Bledsoe, the man Brady had replaced as starting quarterback five months earlier.

Bledsoe performed ably and admirably, completing the drive Brady had started with a touchdown that put the Pats ahead 14–3 with halftime approaching and continuing on through the end of the game. But on the whole Bledsoe had about the same degree of success as Brady, which wasn't much and which likely wouldn't have been enough. The Pats' two quarterbacks combined for just 217 passing yards and a single touchdown on the day. Passes to Brown accounted for 121 of those yards.

And the play that sealed the win and a trip to Super Bowl XXXVI for New England once again turned on Brown's outstanding play on special teams.

Midway through the third quarter, Steelers kicker Kris Brown's 34-yard field goal attempt came out low enough for Patriots defensive tackle Brandon Mitchell to get a hand on the ball. Brown grabbed the loose ball and started downfield, only to be snagged by the kicker at the Pittsburgh 49-yard line. But in a heads-up move that might have gone terribly wrong if it had been attempted by a less experienced player, Brown lateraled to defensive back Antwan Harris, who carried the ball into the end zone.

The Patriots would give up touchdowns on each of Pittsburgh's next two offensive possessions, but it wouldn't be enough. New England would come out ahead 24–17.

And while Bledsoe would garner most of the postgame attention—partly due to sentiment, partly to the idea that a pre-Super Bowl quarterback controversy might emerge—even he knew it was really Brown's efforts on special teams that had made the difference.

"If there's a more valuable player in the league to his team than Troy Brown, I don't know who it would be," Bledsoe said after the game. "Without Troy Brown, I don't know what our record would be this year, but we would certainly not be standing where we are right now."

Bill Belichick, too, offered high praise. "That guy is some football player," the coach said. "He does the big things, but he does all the little things. You just love to have guys like that on your team."

That's what makes Brown one of those Patriots players who'll never be forgotten.

Brown won't be remembered as potentially the greatest player ever at his position, the way Hannah is. He's not Cappelletti, who helped build the Patriots as a player and coach and then forged a permanent connection with fans while serving as one of the

BLEDSOE'S LAST BLAST

Most Patriots fans had fallen out of love with Drew Bledsoe by the time he took over for an injured Tom Brady in the 2001–02 AFC Championship. There were still a few hard-core Bledsoe loyalists out there, of course. But most knew, as Bledsoe trotted out onto the field late in the second half, that unless Brady's injury was much worse than it looked, they were probably seeing Bledsoe line up under center as a Patriot for the last time. Bledsoe handled his swan song with aplomb, completing 10 of 21 passes for 102 yards and a touchdown. He was awarded a game ball. And, if nothing else, he ended his career in New England on a positive note.

team's chief radio voices for what seems like a thousand years. Nor is he Grogan, who'll be loved forever for his unwavering willingness to give everything he had to his team, regardless of how little it sometimes gave him in return.

Brown played during better times than any of those other quintessential Patriots. He has three rings to show for it. And no one would ever argue that he faced the kind of adversity Patriots players in earlier eras had to endure.

But that doesn't make Troy Brown any less special.

Brown will be remembered not nearly so much for when he played as for how. He'll be recalled forever as a player who did everything his team asked of him—and did it well—every time he took the field. And if history is ultimately just, he'll be remembered for single-handedly getting the Patriots to the first Super Bowl they'd ever win.

NUMBERS DON'T LIE [OR DO THEY?]

THE SYSTEM GUYS: TOM BRADY'S FORMER RECEIVERS

The idea that you can plug virtually any wide receiver into the Patriots offense and turn him into a gamebreaker went out the window on January 21, 2007. Out the window, through Reche Caldwell's outstretched hands, and into the waiting arms of Randy Moss, Wes Welker, and Donté Stallworth.

Give old Ricochet his due. Caldwell probably had as much to do with the astounding success of the Patriots' offense during the 2007 season as anyone in the team's front office. (He certainly had a greater effect on the Pats than any other player who suited up for the Washington Redskins in '07.) Caldwell's drops at crucial moments during the Pats' 38–34 loss to the Indianapolis Colts in the 2006–07 AFC Championship forever put the lie to the notion that all a receiver needs to succeed in the NFL is Tom Brady throwing the ball his way.

It could be mere coincidence that the Pats brought in four new receivers through free agency and trades in the three months following that heartbreaking loss—and that Caldwell was the odd man out when the Pats found themselves loaded at the position in training camp—but that doesn't seem a likely explanation.

Still, if 2006 proved that you can't just have Brady throw balls at tree trunks and expect them to stick, then 2007 proved something else: give Brady the best receiving corps in the league and you end up with an offense that shatters records. And that in turn underscores a meaningful point: those other guys, the ones who signed big contracts with various other teams after benefiting from Brady's abilities for a few seasons are talented enough, but leaving New England they were all at least overvalued and probably overrated.

Take Deion Branch, the Patriots' top receiver in 2003 and 2005 and the MVP of Super Bowl XXXIX (in which he caught a record-tying 11 passes for 133 yards). Branch held out in the 2006 preseason and into the first week of the regular season, finally forcing the Patriots to deal him to the Seattle Seahawks for a first-round pick in the 2007 draft. That situation left New England with a group of receivers—Caldwell, Jabar Gaffney, and (temporarily) Doug Gabriel—any of whom would have made a good second or third option, but none of whom was cut out to be any quarterback's primary target.

Branch's holdout grew out of a demand that the Pats renegotiate his rookie contract, which he was a season away from playing out. What's more, he wanted compensation similar to what the Colts' Reggie Wayne was being paid: about $40 million over six years. And that's in essence what he finally received from the Seahawks (it was $39 million, $13 million of which was guaranteed), who also sacrificed a first-round draft pick to obtain his rights.

BRADY'S MOST UNDERRATED RECEIVER

Can you really call a pass catcher who's made only 10 receptions over seven seasons for a grand total of 68 yards underrated? You can when he's a linebacker. Mike Vrabel, who's sometimes called on to line up at tight end in goal-line situations, has caught 10 passes, all of them for touchdowns, including two in Super Bowls. His career year as a receiver came in 2005 when he snagged three TDs. Another thing about Vrabel: until he started gaining attention in 2007 when he was selected for the Pro Bowl for the first time in his 11-year career, he was also underrated as a linebacker.

But Branch has never been Wayne. Although the two wide-outs put up similar numbers in 2005 (Branch caught 78 passes for 998 yards; Wayne caught 83 for 1,055; both caught five touchdowns), Branch did it as the primary target in an offense that accumulated 4,120 yards through the air while Wayne did it as the secondary target in an offense that put up 4,096 passing yards. And whereas 2005 was a career season for Branch, it wasn't for Wayne, who had 77 catches for 1,210 yards and 12 TDs in 2004. In fact, 2005 was the only season in his career in which Branch had managed numbers on par with Wayne's.

So even if the Pats operated with the same philosophy of player management as the Colts—they don't; Indy concentrates its cap allocation on its top skill players, while New England spreads its money around more evenly—it would have come as no great shock that the Patriots were unwilling to offer Branch a Wayne-type contract.

That's not to say Branch's production in New England wasn't good. It was. But it clearly wasn't worth what Branch thought. Not to the Pats, anyhow.

The Seahawks obviously disagreed. And the question of whether they were right has yet to be answered—though things aren't looking good.

Branch's total output in Seattle has been disappointing. He contributed 725 yards on 53 catches in 2006 and 661 yards on 49

BRADY'S OTHER MOST UNDERRATED RECEIVER

Kevin Faulk is underrated pretty much across the board. Though the versatile tailback rarely gets much notice, he's been a key contributor to the Patriots for nine seasons. Faulk has a career average of 3.8 yards a carry. He's the team's all-time kickoff return leader, with 3,918 yards and two touchdowns to his credit. And he's been consistent and reliable catching passes out of the backfield. Faulk has recorded 323 career catches for 2,818 yards and 11 touchdowns. In 2003 he caught more passes than David Givens and David Patten combined, finishing second to Deion Branch in total receptions.

catches in 2007, scoring four TDs each year. But he played one short season (he wasn't traded until the '06 campaign was under way) and missed five games due to injury in the other.

Branch may yet prove to be the player Seattle paid for, but it probably won't be in 2008. Branch tore an ACL in the Seahawks' 2007–08 divisional playoff loss to the Green Bay Packers and, as this book went to press, was expected to miss at least the first two weeks of the season.

Meanwhile Randy Moss, who cost the Patriots all of $5 million in 2007, caught 98 passes for 1,493 yards and 23 touchdowns (Branch caught 14 TDs in four seasons in New England). He did it playing in the same offense Branch played in but with a stronger group of receivers to compete with for passes. And Welker caught a team record 112 passes for 1,175 yards and eight touchdowns (three more than Branch managed in his best season). He did that operating out of the slot. And he did it on a five-year, $18 million contract.

That defines value.

What's truly incredible, however, is that Branch might well be the least compelling example of an ex-Patriot receiver failing to deliver for his next team.

Better to look at David Givens, New England's top receiver during the 2004 campaign (during which Branch spent several games sidelined with a knee injury). Givens pulled down 56 balls for 874 yards and three touchdowns in his best season as a Patriot. He was a solid producer for New England again in 2005, setting him up to sign a five-year, $24 million contract with the Tennessee Titans in 2006.

It's impossible to measure Givens' season-by-season output for the Titans against what he managed with the Pats because he tore an ACL 10 weeks into his first year with Tennessee and hasn't played a down since. But it's worth noting that Givens, who played only four complete games for the Titans in the 10 weeks he was on the team's active roster, saw his yards per game dip from 57 in his final season with the Pats to 21 with the Titans (25 factoring out the game in which he was hurt).

It's also worth looking at David Patten, who parlayed his success during four seasons with the Patriots (the right four:

Patten has three rings) into a five-year, $13 million deal with the Washington Redskins in 2005. Washington gave Patten $3.5 million up front.

Like Givens, Patten never played a complete season for the team that signed him away from New England. He suffered a knee injury that required surgery nine games into his first season in Washington. His production to that point, however, had dipped considerably from what it had been with the Patriots. Patten was averaging 24 yards per game in Washington, down from 50 his last season in New England.

In 2006 Patten fell down the Redskins' depth chart. He never started a game, played in only five, and caught just one pass (though it went for 25 yards).

Released by Washington during the 2007 off-season, Patten signed a one-year deal with New Orleans for the 11-year veteran player minimum salary of $820,000. He had something of a renaissance with the Saints. Teamed with Drew Brees, Patten caught 54 passes for 792 yards and three touchdowns, making him, dollar-for-dollar, the best deal in former Patriots wideouts.

Caldwell, Brady's main target in 2006, signed a one-year deal with the Redskins after he was released by the Patriots. He caught 15 passes for 141 yards in eight games with Washington, operating as the third option on most plays. Caldwell was thrown to four times, but made just one catch for seven yards in the Redskins' 35–14 wild-card playoff loss to the Seahawks.

BEHIND THE LINE: DANTE SCARNECCHIA

Think about how many times you've heard one of these lines from a game analyst: "Tom Brady's getting great protection." "Brady's taking his time, waiting for his receivers to get open." Or best yet, "Brady's got all day in the pocket."

You know what happens to wideouts when they leave New England. And two of the receivers who joined the Pats in 2007, Randy Moss and Wes Welker, had career seasons. All of that could be chalked up to Brady, who's poised and smart and has great presence and amazing accuracy. But that wouldn't be telling the whole story. Nor would it be enough to state simply that Brady has, through most of his career, played behind one of the best offensive lines in football.

He has. And during the 2007 season it became impossible not to notice.

But the point is, that line didn't just pop into existence. The Pats' front office during the Belichick era has demonstrated an uncanny ability to identify great offensive line prospects. And the team's philosophy of spreading out its salary cap allocation has helped it retain top talent and given the Pats' depth in the trenches.

More than anything else, however, New England's stellar O line play has come about as the result of the incredible job assistant head coach/offensive line coach Dante Scarnecchia has done helping players make the difficult transition from college- to

Patriots assistant head coach/ offensive line coach Dante Scarnecchia is seen before the game with the New York Jets in Foxborough, Massachusetts, on Sunday, December 4, 2005. The Patriots defeated the Jets 16–3.

pro-style blocking and adapting the Pats' line play to the specific skills of the guys who operate behind it.

Scarnecchia, who has been coaching in the NFL for 26 years (24 of them in New England), is one of the league's hidden gems, an assistant coach who does his job expertly and elevates the play of the athletes he works with but who never steps into the spotlight. Kind of like the offensive linemen he coaches.

Sometimes, though, a player—or a group of players—performs so well that it becomes impossible not to notice them. And in 2007 there was no way to watch New England closely without recognizing what Scarnecchia's players contributed to the team's record-breaking success.

In play after play, as the Patriots passed their way to unprecedented offensive numbers, Brady could be seen hanging in the pocket for what seemed like an eternity, waiting for one receiver or another to beat coverage. You'd see pass rushers clamoring to break through or blitzers trying hard to get around the edges. And you'd see Brady, bouncing slightly, waiting, waiting, stepping up into the pocket, then firing downfield to Moss or finding Welker crossing underneath.

You only occasionally saw Brady hurried, rarely saw him flushed out of the pocket, and almost never saw him take a sack.

Brady was the most frequently blitzed quarterback in the NFL in 2007. Opposing defenses sent extra pass rushers after Brady on 37 percent of the Patriots' pass plays. And still Brady took only 21 sacks, the fifth fewest in the league. More to the point, Brady took those 21 sacks while attempting 578 passes. That's one sack for every 27.5 times he dropped back.

And the same line that kept Brady safe while he put up a league-best 4,806 yards and posted an NFL-record 50 passing touchdowns also opened the holes through which the Pats' running backs dashed for 1,849 yards and 17 touchdowns. Linemen did it by constantly adapting their play on the fly in order to accommodate running back Laurence Maroney's slashing running style. Although Maroney's increasing output as the season wore on was typically attributed to defenses committing more players to stopping the pass, it also had to do with the Pats'

BEHIND THE CAMERA: STEVE SCARNECCHIA

Matt Estrella, the Patriots' video assistant whose work was at the heart of the Spygate incident, didn't invent his own techniques for taping opposing teams' signals. Estrella trained in the Patriots' video department with Steve Scarnecchia, the son of assistant head coach/offensive line coach Dante. In 2005 Steve left the Pats to take over as video director for the New York Jets under Eric Mangini. Any guesses what his duties there include?

O line becoming ever more adept at the blocking techniques needed to open holes suited to Maroney's abilities and style, which differ significantly from the straight-ahead running Corey Dillon had practiced for the three seasons prior to '07.

The line also paved the way for New England's 48-percent conversion rate on third downs, the second-best mark in football.

New England sent three offensive linemen to the Pro Bowl in 2007: left tackle Matt Light, left guard Logan Mankins, and center Dan Koppen. Had right guard Stephen Neal and right tackle Nick Kaczur stayed healthy through the season (both were in and out of the lineup with nagging injuries), the Pats' starting offensive line might easily have gone to Hawaii as a complete unit. (And fortunately, the team's backups, particularly center/guard Russ Hochstein and tackle Ryan O'Callaghan, always manage to perform admirably when they're needed, another tribute to Scarnecchia.)

It's not easy to see great play that typically happens away from the ball, particularly when watching football on TV (the eye naturally follows the football; the camera *has* to). But Randy Cross says it's not too hard to understand what great line play is. Cross, who spent 13 years on the line for the San Francisco 49ers and has three rings to show for it, has watched the Pats closely in his career as a broadcaster. In addition to his work with CBS TV during the season and as a host on Sirius NFL Radio, Cross serves as a game analyst for local broadcasts of Patriots preseason games.

WITH THE GREATEST OF EASE

Sam Cunningham never needed the Patriots' offensive line to open a hole for him. At least not at the goal line. All Sam "Bam" needed O linemen to do was duck. The 6'2", 233-pound fullback's signature move was a head-first leap over the line and into the end zone. It made him famous at USC. And it made him fun to watch in his nine seasons with the Pats. That wasn't all Cunningham could do, however. Twenty-six years after he retired, Randall's big brother is still New England's all-time rushing leader with 5,453 yards. (The top active rusher is Kevin Faulk with 2,666.)

"The fact that you're able to run the ball when you need to run the ball, throw the ball and protect whenever you need to do that, and you're able to turn it off and on, that doesn't happen by mistake," Cross says.

If an offense is clicking, linemen are doing their jobs well. If it's clicking at a record pace, linemen are doing their jobs exceptionally well.

Scarnecchia has been with the Patriots for all but two years since he joined Ron Meyer's staff in 1982. He took over coaching duties for the Pats' O line in 1999. But it's been under Belichick, who elevated Scarnecchia to assistant head coach as soon as he arrived in Foxborough in 2000, that Scarnecchia has had his greatest success.

That's partially an outgrowth of player selection, but Cross says it's also a reflection of the fact that Scarnecchia's coaching style is perfectly suited to the way Belichick runs his team.

"Bill Belichick insists on that attention to detail, that attention to fundamentals and technique," Cross says. "When you have a Dante Scarnecchia, you don't have to worry about that. You get that anyway."

And as much as Belichick has helped spur Scarnecchia's success, Cross says, the relationship also works the other way around.

"You can't tell me there's a single head coach in the Hall of Fame who doesn't have at least a handful of assistant coaches who should be in there with him," Cross says. "Dante's one of those guys."

FINALLY A HALL OF FAMER: ANDRE TIPPETT

Andre Tippett's election to the Pro Football Hall of Fame came about nine years later than it should have. But it came. On February 2, 2008, as the team he gave his heart and soul to during its darkest period prepared to play in its fourth Super Bowl in seven years, Tippett was elected as a member of the Hall of Fame's class of 2008. The fact that he should have been a member of the class of 1999 hardly seemed to matter. Fourteen years after Tippett's career ended, professional football had finally seen fit to recognize one of its overlooked greats.

In his humbly titled 2007 book, *The Paolantonio Report*, ESPN's Sal Paolantonio named Tippett the most underrated pass rusher of all time. Paolantonio compared Tippett favorably to his better-known contemporary, Lawrence Taylor.

Tippett, he wrote, "had the misfortune of playing virtually his entire career in anonymity in Foxboro [sic], Massachusetts, at the same time as Lawrence Taylor was busy becoming the most famous football player in the world." While Taylor's inspired play made headlines in New York, Paolantonio wrote, Tippett compiled a similarly impressive set of statistics while operating way below the radar in New England.

Paolantonio is right about the stats and accordingly correct in his contention that Tippett should have been inducted into the Pro Football Hall of Fame the same year as Taylor. Both players retired after the 1993 season. Taylor made the Hall of Fame on his first ballot in 1999. Tippett never received consideration until 2007.

It's possible, however, that Tippett would have been overlooked even if he hadn't played in New England.

Yes, the Patriots were 80–104 during Tippett's 11 seasons in Foxborough. Yes, they recorded two of the worst seasons in team history late in that stretch, finishing 1–15 in 1990 and a 2–14 in 1992. And yes, the team never posted more than six wins in any of Tippett's last five seasons.

Former Patriots linebacker Andre Tippett stands for photographs after being announced as the newest Pro Football Hall of Fame inductee on February 2, 2008.

But Tippett also was a member of the 1985 team that was the first Patriots squad to make the Super Bowl. In fact, he had one of his best seasons in 1985, recording 16.5 sacks and making one of his two career touchdowns on a fumble recovery. He also played well in 1986, a season when the Pats were very much in the national spotlight thanks to their Super Bowl appearance and in which the team won 11 games.

Tippett didn't receive much recognition outside of New England even then. That was partly because the team played in the then-weak AFC. But it was also because Tippett was the kind of player who believed in keeping his head down and doing his job. (He'd have been a great fit in the Bill Belichick era.)

Tippett worked hard. He trained in karate in an effort to gain a competitive edge. And unlike Taylor—who became complacent during his career, convinced his natural ability would always pull him through—Tippett was a warrior from his first game in 1982 until his 151st in 1993.

Playing on the strong side in a 3–4 defense in an era in which tight ends were more typically used as blockers than pass catchers, Tippett still found a way to make 100 sacks, including 35 in 1984 and 1985, which still ranks as the highest two-season sack total by a linebacker in league history. And for all the lack of hype surrounding him, he still managed to qualify for the Pro Bowl five times and to be named Defensive Player of the Year in 1985.

Tippett forced opposing offenses to game plan for him in an effort to keep him away from their quarterbacks. He made things easier on every other member of the Pats' defensive front, consistently drawing double and triple teams. And he still managed to get around blockers and wreak havoc in the backfield.

He also gave Patriots fans someone to cheer for through several seasons during which there was close to nothing to feel good about.

So, sure, Tippett's election to the Hall of Fame was late in coming. It was almost to be expected. Tippett, after all, was almost always underrated everywhere else—even if he was never underrated, or underappreciated, in New England.

DRAFT DAY

ALMOST THE WORST OF A GREAT CLASS: TONY EASON

Every team in the NFL has made its share of draft day mistakes over the years. Every team in the league missed at least two opportunities to draft Joe Montana in 1979 and five to take Tom Brady in 2000.

And first round busts are a dime a dozen. The Patriots have had more than a few over the 48 years they've been in business. (Unless you happen to feel good about the way things worked out with Lester Williams and Eugene Chung.) The Detroit Lions seem somehow to manage one virtually every April.

And yet it's arguable that there's never been a bust/blunder combination as powerful, painful, and, in the minds of fans, unforgivable as the one that brought Tony Eason to New England in 1983.

It would be bad enough if Eason had simply stunk. Or if it should have been evident to then-Patriots personnel director Dick Steinberg that he was going to stink. It was beyond bad enough, considering he was brought in to replace Steve Grogan, one of the toughest, most highly regarded quarterbacks in Patriots history.

But that wasn't the whole of it—not by a long shot. Because Eason was a part of the now-famous Class of '83, the draft that brought John Elway, Jim Kelly, Ken O'Brien, and Dan Marino into the NFL. And while the Patriots, who drafted 15th overall that year, never had a shot at Elway (first) or Kelly (14th), they took Eason ahead of both O'Brien, who would become a two-time Pro Bowl selection, and Marino, who would go down as one of the best passers in the history of the game.

The only way the Patriots could have done worse in selecting a quarterback in that draft would have been if they'd taken Todd Blackledge. And who knows? Maybe they would have if they'd had a chance. Fortunately Blackledge went to Kansas City at pick number seven, sparing Steinberg a difficult choice.

In fairness to Steinberg, Eason's problem wasn't really that he *couldn't* play his position well. It's that he *wouldn't*.

Eason had an amazingly accurate arm when he was on his game, as he demonstrated during his first year as a starter in 1984 when he managed a 60-percent completion ratio, put up 3,228 yards in 13 starts, and threw 23 touchdowns to just eight interceptions.

Under the right circumstances Eason might have had a standout career. Unfortunately for Eason, playing under the right circumstances would have meant playing flag football. (Or considering Robert Edwards's fate, maybe two-hand touch.)

John Hannah, the great offensive guard, may have wronged Eason when he remarked that the quarterback "should have worn a skirt" (Hannah could certainly have picked a less sexist way to express himself), but the frustration that led to the statement certainly had a foundation in fact. Eason revealed himself to be something of a delicate flower while he was still in college. Long before Steinberg saw fit to draft him, Eason had established a reputation for taking himself out of games in order to recover after taking any kind of meaningful hit. And while there doubtlessly are jobs in the world in which such a strong sense of self-preservation would be considered an asset, NFL quarterback has never been one of them.

Eason never learned to suck it up and take a hit, either. Early on in his six-season (plus three games) tenure with the Pats, Eason reportedly told Grogan, among others, that his goal was to avoid taking the kind of punishment nearly every NFL player endures because he wanted to be sure he'd be pain free and able to play tennis at age 40.

AND TO THINK, THEY GOT BRADY IN ROUND SIX

In the 48-year history of the team, the Patriots have selected a quarterback in the first round of the AFL or NFL draft on four occasions. Only one of those choices, Drew Bledsoe, worked out. For the Pats, anyhow.

Jack Concannon was taken with the first overall pick in the 1964 AFL draft, but the Pats lost a bidding war with the Philadelphia Eagles, who had taken Concannon in the second round of the NFL draft that year. It was just as well. Though he shone bright at Boston College, Concannon was average at best as a pro.

Jim Plunkett went to the Pats as the first overall pick in the 1971 NFL draft. He was murdered behind New England's one-man offensive line for five seasons, then went on to win two Super Bowls with the Oakland/Los Angeles Raiders.

Then there was Tony Eason.

In Super Bowl XX, he was visibly intimidated by the Chicago Bears defense. He was hardly unusual in that regard; the Bears' vaunted 46 defense was, in many ways, designed to put the fear of God in quarterbacks. But Eason fell apart in the face of that D on the game's biggest stage, turning in the worst performance by a quarterback in Super Bowl history.

And as the seasons wore on, Eason's distaste for the physical aspects of football became more and more evident. He developed a noticeable tendency to audible to handoffs whenever an opposing defense showed blitz, shifting the likelihood of pain to the Patriots' running backs.

And although Eason led the Patriots to an 11–5 finish and a playoff berth in 1986—a feat he and Grogan managed in tandem just as they'd done in '85—his teammates favored Grogan. So did the fans.

In 1987 hometown hero Doug Flutie came along for his first stint with the Pats (with the memory of his Heisman

Trophy–winning senior year at Boston College and its associated heroics still fresh in every New Englander's mind) and the fans wanted him.

Eason started just three games in 1987 and two in 1988. He opened the 1989 season as the Pats' chosen starter, but the designation wouldn't stick.

Eason played relatively well in an opening day win over the New York Jets in the Meadowlands, throwing for 273 yards and a pair of touchdowns. But he managed only one touchdown a week later in a home loss to the Miami Dolphins and none in a week-three loss in Foxborough to the Seattle Seahawks. The defining moment of Eason's season, and probably the last straw in the eyes of fans, came in that Seattle game. On a third-and-six, with the pocket crumbling, Eason scrambled toward the Patriots' sideline. It appeared he would pick up a first down, but at the last second he pulled up and threw the ball over the head of wide receiver Stanley Morgan, who was operating in tight double coverage. The crowd booed. And whether fans were right or wrong in the perception that Eason had once again chosen to spare himself at the team's expense, there was no questioning that the quarterback had made his own bed.

Eason was benched. Then eight weeks into the season he was told that if he wanted to stay with the team he would have to renegotiate his $1.1 million salary. Under the new terms laid out by the Patriots, Eason would be paid only if he took more than half the snaps in each week's game. Otherwise he'd get nothing.

When Eason balked at that deal, as general manager Pat Sullivan must have known he would, he was waived.

Shockingly Eason was claimed off waivers by the Jets. After pondering his options for two weeks (a move that was perceived as a stall Eason used to stay out of pads until after New York's week nine meeting with New England), he reported. He started two games in relief of Ken O'Brien, then spent the 1990 season riding the pine. And there his career came to a close—with about as much fanfare and excitement as Eason was ever worth.

OVERALL PICK #199: TOM BRADY

Let's run it down, just for the record.

Tom Brady was the 199th overall selection in the 2000 NFL draft, taken by the Patriots with the 33rd pick in the sixth round. One of two compensatory picks the Pats had been granted at the end of the sixth, the selection that brought Brady to New England was the team's second overall in the round.

Brady was the seventh quarterback taken that year. The first six: Chad Pennington, first round (18th overall) by the New York Jets; Giovanni Carmazzi, third round, San Francisco 49ers; Chris Redman, third round, Baltimore Ravens; Tee Martin, fifth round, Pittsburgh Steelers; Marc Bulger, sixth round, New Orleans Saints; Spergon Wynn, sixth round, Cleveland Browns.

The 2007 season was Bulger's sixth as a starter. It also saw Pennington demoted to backing up Kellen Clemens and Redman falling third on the Atlanta Falcons' depth chart.

Carmazzi, Martin, and Wynn are out of the NFL, never having made a mark—or, in the case of Carmazzi and Martin, so much as started a game.

And Brady—the skinny kid who split time at quarterback with Drew Henson at the University of Michigan and impressed almost no one at the 2000 NFL scouting combine with his 5.23-second 40 time and 24.5 inch vertical leap—has gone on to become arguably the best quarterback in NFL history.

It's a good thing for the Patriots that Bill Belichick and Scott Pioli saw it coming.

Except that they didn't. Not really. Which is why the Pats took tackles Adrian Klemm and Greg Robinson-Randall, running back J.R. Redmond, tight end Dave Stachelski, defensive end Jeff Marriott, and cornerback Antwan Harris ahead of Brady. (Not one of those players remains on the team.)

That said, Brady didn't exactly fall in the Patriots' laps. He was on Belichick's radar screen coming out of college. And it can't possibly surprise anyone at this point that Belichick went into the 2000 draft, his first as the Patriots' head coach, only after substantial preparation. Nor should it come as a shock that it was that preparation, not luck, that made Brady a Patriot.

Patriots quarterback and Super Bowl XXXVI Most Valuable Player Tom Brady speaks to reporters on February 4, 2002, in New Orleans.

When Belichick arrived in Foxborough, he recognized that he had his work cut out for him. The Pats had not managed their money or the salary cap well in the three years since Belichick had departed along with Bill Parcells for the New York Jets. The Pats were thin on talent, and with a $10 million cap deficit looming for the 2000 season they were on the verge of getting thinner still.

The team's quarterback situation, beyond Drew Bledsoe, was troublesome. Belichick wanted a solid backup for his starting quarterback who was talented, but hideously immobile (read: destined to get his clock cleaned but good eventually). And he knew he was going to have to at least try to find one in the draft.

Belichick sent Dick Rehbein, the quarterbacks coach he'd hired away from the New York Giants, to scout two potential QBs: Louisiana Tech's Tim Rattay and Michigan's sometimes-starter Brady.

Rehbein liked Rattay. He loved Brady.

IT'S BETTER TO BE LUCKY THAN GOOD

While it wasn't pure happenstance that led the Patriots to draft Tom Brady, it's probably not the best idea to hold up the star QB as evidence of Bill Belichick and Scott Pioli's draft-day genius. Pioli certainly doesn't. The Pats' vice president of player personnel keeps on his desk a football card that features both Brady and Dave Stachelski, the tight end New England took in the fifth round of the 2000 draft, 58 picks ahead of Brady. Stachelski didn't make the team. "If we thought he was going to be that good I don't think we'd have waited until the 199th pick," Pioli has said.

Scouting Brady, Rehbein found that the quarterback whose physical abilities were being routinely questioned by scouts and draft experts, usually to the exclusion of all other considerations, brought several other assets to the table. Brady was smart—a high scorer on the Wonderlic Assessment Test with a great football IQ and disciplined study habits that had him on track to graduate with honors. He was a leader, a player whose teammates universally said he brought out the best in them on the field. And he was a natural competitor who thrived under pressure.

Rehbein told Belichick that if he was going to take a quarterback in the draft, it should be Brady. Having paid attention to Rehbein's scouting reports and to Brady's performance in the Orange Bowl, in which he led Michigan to an overtime win over Alabama with 369 passing yards and four touchdowns, Belichick concurred.

And on April 16, 2000, as the draft headed toward its final round, the Pats looked at a board that included both Brady and Rattay, and they grabbed Brady.

The wisdom of that selection wouldn't begin to make itself known in any real sense for another 17 months. But hints started showing up fairly quickly.

Brady became known in Foxborough as the hardest-working player on the team. He did all the things players are supposed to do but that few rarely do: he came in early and went home late.

He worked out hard and studied harder. He became friendly with everyone on the team. And he approached every task assigned to him as if it were make or break.

As the fourth quarterback on the depth chart in 2000, Brady had the task of running the scout team—the squad charged with running the following week's opponent's offense in practice to help the defensive starters prepare. His embrace of the job became legendary. Every week Brady learned a new offense and ran it so well that Patriots defenders rarely saw anything that surprised them on game days. After practice, Brady would keep the scout team together and work on his own team's offense. He wasn't just preparing himself for the possibility that he might one day have to start for the Patriots, he was preparing the players around him for the same possibility. He was improving the Patriots' depth at every offensive position.

Belichick had gotten more than he'd counted on out of his sixth-round draft choice before the 2000 season concluded. And Brady's real value hadn't yet begun to show.

Even in 2001, as he led the team to six straight wins down the stretch, turning a 5–5 team into the AFC's second playoff seed, then on to an upset victory in Super Bowl XXXVI, Brady didn't establish himself as one of the greats. He showed incredible poise for a first-year starter and the best leadership skills the Pats had seen from a quarterback since Steve Grogan, but those things alone don't make great quarterbacks. Neither did becoming the youngest quarterback to win a Super Bowl and the second-youngest player (after Pittsburgh Steelers wide receiver Lynn Swann) to be named Super Bowl MVP.

Brady's numbers in 2001 were good but not earth shattering. His 63.9 percent completion rate was excellent, but not as good as the numbers put up by the St. Louis Rams' Kurt Warner or the Oakland Raiders' Rich Gannon, both of whom finished with higher completion ratios while putting up 130 more pass attempts than Brady. And his 18-to-12 touchdown-to-interception ratio revealed some need for improvement.

Still, it was clear before Super Bowl XXXVI kicked off—much less before Brady led the impressive nine-play, 53-yard drive that

BRADY OR MANNING?

Though they entered the NFL under completely different circumstances—one as a much ballyhooed first overall pick in the 1998 draft, the other as an afterthought sixth-rounder two years later—Peyton Manning and Tom Brady have proven to be the top two quarterbacks of their era. And since they'll always be compared, here's how they stack up:

	Manning	Brady
Career passer rating	94.7	92.9
Career completion percentage	64.2	63.0
Touchdowns per season	30.6	28.1
Regular season record	105–55	86–24
Regular season winning percentage	.656	.782
Pro Bowl selections	8	4
Times named league MVP	2	1
Playoff record	7–7	14–3
Playoff winning percentage	.500	.824
Super Bowls won	1	3
Super Bowl MVP	1	2

put the team within range for the winning field goal in the final seconds of the game—that the sixth-round draft choice (not the first overall pick he'd been brought in to back up) represented the team's best hope for the future.

Eleven weeks after that Super Bowl, Drew Bledsoe was headed to Buffalo, and Tom Brady was headed for the history books.

Within three years Brady would be a two-time Super Bowl MVP and three-time champion. In his first seven years as a starter, he would go to the Pro Bowl four times.

And in the 2007 season, playing with a group of elite receivers for the first time in his career, he set the league on fire, completing a record 50 touchdown passes, while throwing only eight interceptions. Brady passed for 4,806 yards in 2007, completing

398 of 578 pass attempts for a completion ratio of 68.9 percent, and posting a passer rating of 117.2 (second only to Peyton Manning's 2004 mark of 121.1). He led his team to the first 16–0 regular-season record in NFL history and to a record-shattering 589 points. Not surprisingly, he was named league MVP for the first time in his career.

Brady's career accomplishments in the postseason were even more astounding. His record as a starter in the playoffs through the end of the 2007–08 postseason was 14–3. And in those 17 playoff outings, which included five conference championship games and four Super Bowls, he threw 26 touchdowns to just 12 interceptions. He holds the league record for highest completion percentage in a playoff game, having connected on 26 of 28 passes (92.9 percent) in New England's 2007–08 divisional round win over the Jacksonville Jaguars. He holds the record for most completions in the Super Bowl, with 32 in Super Bowl XXXVIII. And he holds the record for most consecutive postseason wins: 10.

The argument about who is the best quarterback in NFL history may prove impossible to resolve, though Brady certainly will always be one of the top contenders. But if there were ever an argument to be had about the greatest ever draft bargains, it was settled by the time Brady led the Pats to their second Super Bowl victory. And overall pick #199 just keeps getting harder to top.

BUILDING THROUGH THE DRAFT

Drafting NFL players is an inexact science to say the least. But it's hard to argue with many of the picks made during the Bill Belichick/Scott Pioli era. Take these, for example:

- 2000—Tom Brady (sixth round); Patrick Pass (seventh round).
- 2001—Richard Seymour (first round); Matt Light (second round).
- 2002—Daniel Graham (first round); Deion Branch (second round); Jarvis Green (fourth round); David Givens (seventh round).

- 2003—Ty Warren (first round); Eugene Wilson (second round); Dan Klecko (fourth round); Asante Samuel (fourth round); Dan Koppen (fifth round).
- 2004—Vince Wilfork (first round); Benjamin Watson (first round).
- 2005—Logan Mankins (first round); Ellis Hobbs (third round); Nick Kaczur (third round).
- 2006—Laurence Maroney (first round); Stephen Gostkowski (fourth round); Ryan O'Callaghan (fifth round).
- 2007—Brandon Meriweather (first round).

THE RIGHT CHOICE: DREW BLEDSOE OVER RICK MIRER

It wasn't always so clear. There was a time, and it was a longer stretch than many fans remember, when there was doubt about whether Bill Parcells had made the right choice with his first draft pick as head coach of the Patriots.

There was doubt even before the pick was made. Drew Bledsoe or Rick Mirer. If you had assembled a jury of Pats fans off the street (assuming you could still find 12 people willing to admit they were fans of a team that hadn't managed to sniff .500 in four seasons) and presented a case for both quarterbacks, you'd have ended up with an even half dozen on each side.

The debate had come alive virtually the moment the Pats announced the hiring of Parcells. The team was coming off one of the worst seasons in its history. The Pats had finished the 1992 season 2–14; as a reward, they would have the first overall pick in the 1993 draft. And there was little doubt that the Pats were going to use the pick on a quarterback. Their top performer in the previous two seasons was Hugh Millen, who managed to throw 17 touchdowns and 28 interceptions in his 20 starts.

The question was whether that pick would be Mirer, a three-year starter at storied Notre Dame with a college record of 29–7–1 and two wins in major bowl games under his belt, or Bledsoe, a junior from Washington State University who put up dizzying numbers (7,373 yards and 44 touchdowns) in 28 starts.

116

There were reasons to like both. Mirer was the more mobile quarterback, the more experienced quarterback, and the kid who had demonstrated an ability to perform well in the big spot. Bledsoe was bigger, had a cannon for an arm, and had played in an offense closer to what he'd be asked to run in the pros than the option-oriented offense Mirer had run under Lou Holtz at Notre Dame.

Depending on your point of view, Parcells either couldn't make the wrong choice or he couldn't make the right one. Then there was the phantom third option. *The Boston Globe* reported just before draft day that the San Francisco 49ers had offered two

Patriots quarterback Drew Bledsoe drops back behind his offensive line after taking the snap in the first quarter of the AFC wildcard playoff game against the Miami Dolphins on December 28, 1997. The Patriots defeated the Dolphins 17–3.

first-round choices, numbers 18 and 27, and a third-rounder for the Patriots' pick. Parcells denied the report, but confirmed that at least one team was interested in trading up for the pick.

Parcells, too, spent some time on the fence. But in the end he elected the player with the arm and the pro-style offense experience over the marquee player.

Eight months later, as the 1993 NFL season came to a close, it was still unclear whether Parcells had made the right decision.

Mirer, chosen by the Seattle Seahawks with the second overall pick in the draft, got off to a solid start in his rookie season. The Seahawks won only six games in 1993, but Mirer set rookie records for pass attempts (486), completions (274), and yards (2,833). He started all 16 games that season and was named AFC Rookie of the Year.

Bledsoe put up respectable numbers as a rookie but started only 12 games, missing four midseason due to a knee injury. The Pats went 5–7 in the games Bledsoe started but were led to victory in one of those by backup Scott Secules.

Bledsoe did come on at the end of the season, however, leading the team on a season-saving four-game winning streak and throwing 27 completions for 329 yards in a 33–27 win over Miami in the season finale. (That win helped endear Bledsoe to Pats fans by eliminating Dan Marino's Dolphins from postseason contention. Schadenfreude was a valuable commodity in the lean years of the late '80s and early '90s.)

The 1994 season would validate Parcells's choice. As the Seahawks once again struggled to a 6–10 record, the Pats turned things around, finishing 10–6 and making their first postseason appearance in eight years. Bledsoe completed 400 passes for 4,555 yards and 25 touchdowns. Mirer managed only half that output (though he started only 13 games). The disparity was again in evidence in 1995. Then, in 1996, the year Bledsoe led the Pats to their second Super Bowl appearance, Mirer and the Seahawks stumbled to a 7–9 record.

That was Mirer's last season with the Seahawks. He bounced around the league for four more seasons but never settled with a team and never started more than eight games in a season.

BETTER LATE THAN ... UMM, NEVER MIND

Rick Mirer wasn't Bill Parcells's top choice in 1993, but he did eventually have the opportunity to start for the legendary coach. Two seasons after he wore out his welcome in Seattle, Mirer landed with the New York Jets, where he started six games for Parcells in place of an injured Vinny Testaverde. Mirer went 2–4 as a Jet and was benched in favor of Ray Lucas.

Bledsoe, of course, wouldn't enjoy what anyone would term a storybook career himself. He'd only ever see the Super Bowl again as a backup to Tom Brady. And by the end of his run in New England, he'd come under constant criticism from fans and the media for, among other things, the very lack of mobility that had led Parcells to look closely at Mirer in 1993. He never seemed to figure out how to read defenses, a skill his replacement has in abundance. And he developed a bad habit of taking sacks. In his last two full seasons taking snaps for the Pats, Bledsoe was sacked 100 times, including a career-high 55 in 1999 (when he was sacked roughly once every 11 times he dropped back to pass).

But in the seven seasons between his rookie campaign and the emergence of Brady in 2001, Bledsoe would perform admirably, sometimes brilliantly. He led the Pats back to the playoffs in each of the two seasons after Parcells ditched the team, despite playing much of the 1998 season with an injured index finger on his throwing hand.

Bledsoe was both liked and admired by his teammates. He was a leader on the field whose cool head helped him engineer 19 fourth-quarter comeback wins during his tenure with the Pats.

"If he has the ball, there doesn't have to be any time on the clock. It could be 0:00 and we'd still win the game," defensive tackle Chad Eaton remarked after Bledsoe pulled off his second consecutive fourth-quarter comeback to open the 1999 season.

And he won the respect of both coaches and ownership. Robert Kraft, who inherited Bledsoe when he purchased the Pats from James Orthwein in 1994, came to look at the quarterback as a son. Moreover, Kraft never really lost faith in Bledsoe. Early in the same year Bledsoe lost his job to Brady, Kraft made him the highest paid player in NFL history at the time with a 10-year, $103 million contract.

"For many reasons, and at many levels, this was a difficult trade to make," Kraft said after the Pats traded Bledsoe to Buffalo in April 2002. "Drew Bledsoe is a special player. I have great respect for all he has done for this franchise, not only for his contributions on the field, but also his contributions off the field. ... He gave our fans some of the greatest memories in the franchise's history and there will always be a special place reserved for him in the hearts of Patriots fans."

Kraft was at least partially right. During his time in Buffalo, Bledsoe always enjoyed a warm welcome in Foxborough.

Still, fans have their own way of remembering things. It's easy now, with Brady setting new standards at the position, to remember Bledsoe for his faults rather than his strengths. And it's probably human nature to remember the disappointing losses with greater clarity than the thrilling wins. So while Bledsoe is universally lauded as a "class act"—a tag he more than earned by keeping his dissatisfaction with losing his job to Brady in 2001 out of the newspapers and then thanking fans for their support as he exited Foxborough—he's too often denied due credit for his talent or his contributions to the team.

Bledsoe never became the best quarterback in Pats history. But he was clearly their best bet in April 1993—and for a good eight seasons thereafter.

ALL HEART—AND THEN SOME

NEVER SAY DIE: STEVE GROGAN

No quarterback was ever tough like Steve Grogan was tough.

Grogan was tough physically, enduring injury after horrible injury during his 16 seasons with the Patriots. And he was tough mentally, bouncing back time and again after being benched, sometimes for the wrong reasons—like when a sexier quarterback, say Tony Eason, landed in Foxborough—and sometimes for the right ones—like when his gunslinger mentality would lead to one interception too many.

He was tough from the moment he showed up as a fifth-round pick in the 1975 draft to the moment he bowed out following the 1990 season.

And although he drove Patriots fans crazy at times, Grogan became a New England sports legend, largely because he was almost always—even when he faced the Chicago Bears' 46 defense in relief of a shell-shocked Eason in Super Bowl XX—one of the two toughest bastards on the field (and second only to John Hannah, the toughest football player who ever lived).

How tough? Grogan endured multiple surgeries: five to clean up and repair his knees (both of them), one to insert a pair of screws into a broken fibula (which was only cracked until Grogan attempted to practice on it), one to reattach a torn tendon in his throwing elbow, and another to remove one of two ruptured disks in his neck. And he kept on playing. Just like he kept on playing after he broke his nonthrowing hand. Just like he kept playing despite suffering cracked ribs, shoulder separations, broken fingers, and (foolishly, given what is known now) no fewer than three concussions.

That tough.

Tough enough that when a defensive player hit him, he sometimes hit back. Tough enough that if opponents tried to advance the ball after a turnover, they could expect him to hit with all the force of a linebacker.

That tough.

"I tried to play like I was a football player and not just a quarterback," Grogan once told *The Boston Globe*. "If I had to deliver a blow, I'd deliver a blow. If I had to run and take the hit, I'd take the hit."

In the black-and-blue world of New England Patriots football of the 1970s and '80s, that alone would have been enough to make Grogan a folk hero.

But that wasn't all there was to Grogan. There was also the fact that when he was good, he was very, very good. Grogan's 26,866 career passing yards are second only to Drew Bledsoe's 29,657 (though it's likely Tom Brady will pass Grogan early in the 2008 season). His 182 passing touchdowns stood as a team record until Brady eclipsed it during his NFL-record-breaking 50-touchdown run in 2007. His 35 career rushing touchdowns are the fourth most by any Patriots player (behind running backs Jim Nance, Sam Cunningham, and Corey Dillon). And his 12 rushing TDs in the 1976 season remain the most by a quarterback in a single season.

Grogan had great mobility before his injuries started piling up. And when he arrived in Foxborough mobility was precisely the quality then-starter Jim Plunkett lacked. Though he was a great passer, Plunkett was a quarterback who would make Drew Bledsoe look like Kordell Stewart. Plunkett, a Heisman Trophy winner and a number one overall draft pick, had turned in a good rookie season with the Pats in 1971 but spent the next three taking a beating behind an offensive line that was shaky at best.

THE OTHERS

Steve Grogan split starts with five quarterbacks beside Jim Plunkett and Tony Eason.

Matt Cavanaugh went 5–10 as a starter between 1980 and '82. He had a long career as a backup QB and assistant coach, and earned Super Bowl rings as a backup with San Francisco and the New York Giants.

Tom Ramsey won two of four starts in 1987 and '88. He was a failure with the Indianapolis Colts in '89.

Doug Flutie was 8–5 as a starter between 1987 and '89. He's considered one of the greatest players in Canadian Football League history. Flutie ended his career back in New England as a backup to Tom Brady.

Marc Wilson won one of 10 games he started for the Pats in 1989 and '90. He came to the Patriots from the Oakland Raiders with two Super Bowl rings, though he never took a snap in either championship game.

Tommy Hodson went 1–11 as a Patriots starter from 1990–92. He later spent time with, but never started for, Miami, Dallas, and New Orleans.

Grogan was seen as a good NFL prospect while quarterbacking the Kansas State University Wildcats. But a neck injury in his senior season raised doubts, causing him to slip considerably in the draft to the point where Patriots coach Chuck Fairbanks was able to snag him in the fifth round.

Fairbanks was elated by the fact that he was able to bring Grogan in. During the Patriots' playoff run in 1976, he told *Time* magazine why in succinct terms: "His eyes light up when it's time to play."

And time to play for the Pats came much earlier than Grogan had expected. Five games into Grogan's rookie season, Fairbanks lost patience with Plunkett and Grogan was elevated to the starting role. The Pats finished 3–11 on the season, but Grogan won the respect of his teammates and fans by displaying an ability to get out of the pocket and a knack for leading by example.

In 1976 Grogan led the potent offense on what is still considered one of the best Patriots teams of all time, an 11–3 squad that might have won the Super Bowl but for one questionable call in a playoff match with the Oakland Raiders.

Teammates still remember the recklessness and disregard for personal safety that inspired them that season.

"Steve Grogan had a chip missing in his internal computer," tight end Russ Francis told *Patriots Gameday* when the team marked the 30th anniversary of the '76 season. "He wouldn't acknowledge that anything was remotely impossible, difficult to do, or dangerous. They invented the quarterback slide because of guys like Steve Grogan."

Grogan lost some of his mobility as the seasons went by, but he never lost his competitive edge. Or his keen understanding of the game.

And in 1979 Grogan's football smarts saw him take on a new role as head coach Ron Erhardt tapped him to call the plays as well as run them.

Grogan enjoyed his best year, statistically speaking, in 1979, passing for 3,286 yards and 28 touchdowns and rushing for two more scores, but the team finished 9–7 and missed the playoffs. It was the last year Grogan would start all of the Pats' games.

He missed four games in 1980 because of knee injuries. Neck and knee injuries caused him to miss nine starts a year later. He was demoted to backing up Matt Cavanaugh for much of the 1982 season, fractured his fibula after getting off to a great start in 1983, and was supplanted by Eason three games into 1984.

It goes on and on from there, right through the end of Grogan's career. He'd come in for a few games, lead the team to a string of victories, and then be lost with a blown knee or a ruptured disk.

Grogan replaced a struggling Tony Eason five games into the 1985 season, leading the team to six consecutive victories and sparking the run that led to a berth in Super Bowl XX. He missed the last five games of the regular season and all of the AFC playoffs due to a broken leg. But he was ready to go for the Super Bowl. And he was sent in to try to salvage the game after Eason spent most of the first half running for his life in the face of the Chicago Bears' pass rush. Grogan completed 17 of 30 passes for 177 yards and a garbage time touchdown, but it wasn't enough. The Pats lost 46–10.

Some fans blamed the Super Bowl loss on coach Raymond Berry's decision to start Eason in that game. Others blamed Eason for failing to play like an NFL quarterback. Others simply recognized that the Pats had run into a buzz saw; the 1985 Bears were, after all, one of the best teams ever to take the field. No one ever blamed Grogan.

Grogan managed just 22 starts over the next five seasons, popping in and out of the lineup. Then, after sitting behind Marc Wilson and Tommy Hodson for most of the Pats' 1–15 1990 season, he called it a career.

Nearly two decades later, with the stands at Gillette Stadium increasingly filled with fans who never saw him take a snap, Grogan is still revered for what he brought to the Patriots—and for the giant chunks of himself that he left on the field.

COMEBACK PLAYER OF THE CENTURY: TEDY BRUSCHI

The image most commonly associated with Tedy Bruschi isn't a football image at all, though it was captured at the site of professional football's biggest game.

It's the image of Bruschi playing with his two young sons, Tedy Jr. and Rex, on the field at Jacksonville's Alltel Stadium hours before Super Bowl XXXIX. In video captured by Fox TV and aired during the pregame show, America saw Bruschi and his four- and two-year-old sons chasing each other, tumbling over the turf together, and laughing as the little guys in their oversized Bruschi game jerseys tackled their dad. Viewers saw Bruschi lift his boys, one in each arm, and plant kisses on their cheeks.

It was a remarkable moment, not because it's unusual to see a father playing with his kids, but because it's unusual to see an NFL linebacker doing much of anything beside doling out punishment on the field. Fox offered the video, in part, because it illustrated how relaxed the Patriots were heading into their third Super Bowl in four years. But it also said something else: it said that in an era in which stories of spoiled sports stars behaving horribly seem to surface daily, there are still at least a few others, champions among them, whose personal lives and priorities are worthy of admiration.

Those images were still very much alive in the minds of Patriots fans 10 days later when news broke that Bruschi had suffered a stroke. And that led many to assume they'd seen the nine-year veteran in pads for the last time in the Pats' victory over the Philadelphia Eagles. (Or, for those few who bothered to watch, in the 2005 Pro Bowl.)

Had that assumption proven accurate, no one would have argued that the Pats could have gotten more for the third-round pick they invested in Bruschi in the 1996 draft.

Bruschi hadn't simply played in four Super Bowls, he'd made significant contributions in three of them. As a rookie, Bruschi sacked Brett Favre twice in Super Bowl XXXI. He made a key stop of Marshall Faulk in the second quarter of Super Bowl XXXVI. And he sacked and intercepted Donovan McNabb in Super Bowl XXXIX.

Patriots linebacker Tedy Bruschi plays with his kids—Tedy Jr., Rex, and Dante—before Super Bowl XLII against the New York Giants at University of Phoenix Stadium on February 3, 2008.

Bruschi had also been a standout in the regular season. Even to this day he remains the only player in NFL history to return four consecutive interceptions for touchdowns and the only Patriots linebacker to return multiple interceptions for touchdowns in a season (something he did in both 2002 and 2003). He logged better than 100 tackles in four of his nine seasons with the team. He was named AFC Defensive Player of the Week four times in 2004, a season in which he emerged as a leader on the Pats' defense.

Beyond the numbers, Bruschi had been a classic blue-collar Patriots player, a guy who rarely missed games due to injury and who was willing to work and contribute wherever he was asked. Though he didn't crack the starting lineup as a linebacker until 1997, he saw action in every game during his rookie season, much of it as a standout on special teams.

In short, Bruschi had done his bit.

And while NFL players had come back from a lot over the years, no one had ever come back from a stroke, mild or otherwise.

With three rings on his fingers and a young family he clearly cared a great deal about at home, Bruschi could have cleaned out his locker and walked away assured of a permanent place in Patriots history and fans' hearts.

He didn't.

In fact, he didn't even sit out a complete season. Although the team initially announced that the minor stroke Bruschi suffered and the surgery to repair the congenital heart defect that had caused it would cause the veteran linebacker to miss all of 2005, Bruschi was fully rehabbed and back on the field by week eight. And it wasn't just for show. Bruschi made 10 tackles in his first game back, a 21–16 victory over the Buffalo Bills in Foxborough. He was named AFC Defensive Player of the Week.

"I just kept getting better. I kept getting stronger," Bruschi said the week he returned to practice. "Workouts improved. Just every day the progress that I made just continued to get better and better, and all of a sudden I came to the point where ... they tell me I can play, I feel like I can play, shoot, I know I can play, so let's just play."

Two years later Bruschi would reveal in his book, *Never Give Up*, that the decision to come back was anything but simple. Even after doctors assured Bruschi his heart defect had been repaired and that playing football would not make him susceptible to a second stroke, he and his wife, Heidi, engaged in significant soul searching before the decision to return was made.

In December 2005, having rounded back into form, he helped turn the Pats' defense into one of the best in the league. At the end of the season he shared NFL Comeback Player of the Year honors with Carolina Panthers wide receiver Steve Smith.

In 2006 Bruschi registered 112 tackles. And in 2007 he quietly led the New England defense with 92 tackles during the team's historic 16–0 run.

Bruschi again asserted his value to the Pats in the run to Super Bowl XLII, making eight tackles in the divisional round win over the Jacksonville Jaguars and another six in the AFC Championship victory over the San Diego Chargers.

The week before Super Bowl XLII, Bruschi told reporters gathered in Arizona he considered his very presence a testament to what stroke survivors can accomplish.

"To help this team get back to this point is a victory for me in itself," Bruschi said. "I have been working with the American Stroke Association a lot and I know this is a victory for all stroke survivors as well."

Off the field Bruschi helps raise funds for stroke research and stroke prevention and treatment education through his organization Tedy's Team. And he continues to be a dedicated family man. His family now includes a fifth member, another son, Dante.

Bruschi most likely will never make the Pro Football Hall of Fame. But he did make football history—and one hell of a lasting impression.

THE GREATEST PATRIOT OF ALL TIME: JOHN HANNAH

Before his career is over, Tom Brady may be widely acknowledged as the best quarterback ever to play the game. (Patriots fans have already called the contest, but a few football experts are still reserving judgment.) But it will be a generation, maybe longer, before anyone in New England gets away with calling Brady the greatest Patriot ever.

That's no slight. Certainly, Brady is as well loved by home fans as any professional athlete could ever hope to be. It's just that the Greatest Patriot title was sewn up before young Tom ever sat on his parents' couch in San Mateo, California, dreaming his first Joe Montana daydream. It belongs now, and for all time (or at least until Pats fans from the '70s and '80s finally go the way of Pat Patriot and the Sullivan family), to John Hannah. Hog. The best offensive lineman ever to squeeze his oversized melon into a helmet. The embodiment of what it means to be a professional football player.

Hannah came to the Patriots as the fourth overall pick in the 1973 draft and stayed until his health would no longer allow him to play at the high level he demanded from himself and everyone around him. He played until there was nothing left of his knees but bone, until team physician Bert Zarins told him to walk away while he could still walk at all. He played through 13 seasons in which his team sometimes flirted with greatness but never achieved it. He played for owners unwilling to make the financial commitment to building a championship squad. He stuck it out through the heartbreak of Super Bowl XX. And through all that time, he never lost the competitive spirit that made him a leader on the field, the intensity that led some teammates to elevate their play but pushed others away, or the ferocity that gave defensive linemen nightmares.

Hannah only missed five games due to injury in a career that spanned 191 regular season and postseason matches. (He missed three others in a 1977 contract dispute.)

He was recognized as All-Pro every year from 1976 through 1985. He was selected to appear in the Pro Bowl in nine of his 13 years. And he was named Offensive Lineman of the Year by the NFL Players Association for four consecutive years from 1978 to 1981.

Hog was enshrined in the Pro Football Hall of Fame in 1991, his first year of eligibility. No one who'd ever seen him play expected

John Hannah, widely considered the greatest Patriot of all time, takes his helmet off for a moment during the January 5, 1986, AFC Divisional Playoff against the Raiders. The Patriots defeated the Raiders 27–20. Photo courtesy of Getty Images.

anything less. For seventeen years, he was the only player in the Hall who spent his entire career with the Patriots.

In 1999 Hannah was recognized by *The Sporting News* as one of the 100 Greatest Football Players, arguably ranking only 20th on the list because of the position he played and the team he played for. Yes, it's true that football games are won and lost in the trenches, but that doesn't change the fact that the TV cameras, and most fans' eyes, follow the ball. Defensive line play draws attention because defensive linemen chase quarterbacks and stuff running backs. Offensive line play tends to go unnoticed except when there's a holding call. (The only O lineman to rank ahead of Hannah on *TSN*'s list is Cincinnati Bengals tackle Anthony Muñoz, who caught seven passes, four of them for touchdowns, during his 13-year career.) And New England in the '70s and '80s was far from the most glamorous place to play professional football.

But Hannah wasn't about glamour, anyway. Even in the years in which he was recognized as the league's top trench warrior (as when *Sports Illustrated* featured him on its cover in 1981, calling him "The Best Offensive Lineman of All Time"), Hannah was a lunch pail–type player, a guy who hit as hard as he could on every snap, in games and in practices alike, because that's what he was paid to do.

Still, it can be hard to understand what it was that made Hannah great if you never had a chance to see him play.

CBS television game analyst Randy Cross, an outstanding guard/tackle who was part of three Super Bowl championship teams during his career with the San Francisco 49ers, says Hannah was an inspiration to him when he entered the NFL in 1976. Cross says understanding Hannah's greatness really just comes down to understanding the physics of sport.

"Hannah would run into somebody—and a *big* somebody— and his feet wouldn't stop; they'd just keep going," Cross says. "It doesn't sound like such a big deal to someone who hasn't done it, but just being able to do that is truly special."

"It's no different if you're smacked in the face with a boxing glove or if you're running full speed for five yards and you run into someone else who's running at you. You've got all that

PATRIOTS HALL OF FAME

John Hannah is one of 11 members of the Patriots Hall of Fame.

The 10 others:
- Bruce Armstrong, offensive tackle, 1987–2000
- Nick Buoniconti, linebacker, 1962–68
- Gino Cappelletti, wide receiver/place-kicker, 1960–70
- Bob Dee, defensive end, 1960–67
- Steve Grogan, quarterback, 1975–90
- Michael Haynes, cornerback, 1976–82
- Jim Lee Hunt, defensive lineman, 1960–70
- Stanley Morgan, wide receiver, 1977–89
- Steve Nelson, linebacker, 1974–87
- Vito "Babe" Parilli, quarterback, 1961–67
- Andre Tippett, linebacker, 1982–93

weight, all that power, all that speed. That adds up to a good amount of force. And the natural instinct when that happens is there will initially be a stop and *then* it's a matter of moving your feet. But if you're able to hit and keep your feet moving like John Hannah was always able to do, that other guy is going in a direction he doesn't want to go in."

Hannah usually kept defensive players moving in the wrong direction, too.

"He was the guy no one wanted to see. Like Joe Greene was the defensive lineman nobody wanted to see," Cross recalls. "You almost had condolences for defensive players. 'Ooh, sorry, you've got John Hannah this week. Oh, that's too bad.'"

Indeed, there came a point in Hannah's career when defenses would shift their best lineman away from him rather than simply allow him to be taken out of a game.

That Hannah's reputation never went to his head is likely a reflection of the point of view that won him such respect to begin with.

Considered a smallish O lineman even for his era at 6'3" and 265 pounds, Hannah labored under the belief that he could only realize his dream of playing on the same level as such childhood heroes as Ray Nitschke, Gale Sayers, and Dick Butkus by investing everything he had in his play. When he knocked defensive linemen on their butts, Hannah wasn't so much proving a point to them as he was to himself.

He expected the same commitment from everyone on his team, particularly the guys manning the line with him. And it produced unmistakable results, as in 1978 when a bruising line led by Hannah opened holes that Patriots rushers exploited to the tune of 3,165 yards. Or in his final season when Hannah, in spite of two injured shoulders and fast-deteriorating knees, played a major role in powering the team to its first Super Bowl appearance.

That intensity also put Hannah at odds with teammates at times. He was particularly brutal in his assessment and treatment of quarterback Tony Eason and center Trevor Matich, first-round picks for the Pats in 1983 and 1985. Hannah considered both players too soft for their jobs, a failing he couldn't forgive.

He also couldn't forgive owner Billy Sullivan whom he believes undermined his own organization's success through cheapness and dishonesty. Hannah's 1977 holdout came after the Sullivans reneged on a deal coach Chuck Fairbanks cut with him and fellow Pro Bowler tackle Leon Gray. Three games later, with the team at 1–2 and the offensive line in disarray, Sullivan caved. Hannah received $165,000 to play the remainder of the season (by way of comparison, the league's top-earning guard in 2007 made approximately $7 million). "He probably could have had me for $135,000 before the season," Hannah told Michael Felger, author of the 2004 team history *Tales From the Patriots Sideline*.

What Hannah never did was hold back when he was on the field. While he may have been unhappy with the things going on around him at times—as with the elevation of Eason to starting QB over tough guy Steve Grogan, the Sullivan family, and even head coach Ron Meyer, whom Hannah so disliked he actually considered early retirement in advance of the 1983 season (a move that might have branded any other player a prima donna, but that, coming from Hannah, only managed to reflect poorly on Meyer)—Hannah continued to wow fans and the media and to energize the team by charging full-on at every opponent every Sunday afternoon.

He was every Patriots fan's favorite player when he announced his retirement in 1986. And he remains every long-time Patriots fan's favorite player 22 years later, in spite of all the recent fireworks.

IT AIN'T OVER 'TIL IT'S OVER

YES, THEY CAN: TOPPLING THE TOP-SEEDED CHARGERS

You don't win games like these. Not often. Almost not ever.

You don't get to have your quarterback throw an interception when you're down eight points with six and a half minutes remaining in a game and somehow end up ahead three points when the clock runs down to nothing.

You don't get to travel across the country to face the best team in your conference, make more mistakes in one game than you normally make in three, and end the day dancing on the home team's field.

And you certainly don't get to do any of those things when the game you're in is a divisional round playoff match and your opponent is coming off a first-round bye. Or when your opponent features the reigning league MVP, more Pro Bowlers than any other team in professional football, and exactly as many All-Pro players as you can count on one hand.

You don't get to do that nine times out of 10. Or 99 times out of 100. Or maybe 999 times out of a 1,000. Or maybe less often than that.

Unless your coach is Bill Belichick and your quarterback is Tom Brady. And unless one of your players is possibly the best defensive back ever to have a standout career as a wide receiver.

The Patriots' 24–21 upset victory over the San Diego Chargers on January 14, 2007, is one of the more astounding postseason

Patriots wide receiver Reche Caldwell hauls in a 49-yard catch to set up the winning field goal in the Patriots' 24–21 victory over the San Diego Chargers in their AFC Divisional Playoff game on January 14, 2007.

feats of the Belichick era. If the Pats had managed to follow the come-from-way-behind win with victories in the AFC Championship a week later and then in Super Bowl XLI, the San Diego game would probably have settled into a place in team lore somewhere just south of the 2001–02 divisional round win over Oakland. That is, it would be talked about forever as one of the best non-Super Bowl events in Patriots history.

Of course, the Patriots didn't win their next game. And with so many great moments to remember from the dynasty years, the 2006–07 playoff matchup likely will only be talked about only as long as the Pats and Chargers continue to meet annually in January. After which it will fade.

Bring the game up, though, 10 or 20 years from now, to someone who was around to watch it, and you'll likely find they have no trouble recalling the match—or at the very least the moment when Troy Brown saved his team from certain defeat.

Because while it's true that Belichick outcoached the Chargers' Marty Schottenheimer that day, effectively ending Schottenheimer's five-year run in San Diego—there was nothing terribly surprising in that.

Yes, Schottenheimer had led his team to a 14–2 regular season record while Belichick's Patriots had only managed a 12–4 finish. That was at least part of the reason the Chargers went into the game favored by four and a half points (that along with the fact that LaDainian Tomlinson had spent the season shattering rushing records and that the Chargers hadn't lost at home all season).

But the teams' records had no bearing on how the coaching matchup would play out when they went head to head.

Other than the fact that they both served stints as defensive coordinator for the New York Giants and head coach of the Cleveland Browns, Belichick and Schottenheimer have next to nothing in common as coaches. Where Belichick's game plans are famously (and for opposing teams, confoundingly) complex, Schottenheimer's can be mind-numbingly simple. More importantly, where Belichick consistently does whatever works, Schottenheimer somehow always manages to panic and do exactly what he shouldn't, which is one of the main reasons his teams always find a way to choke in big games.

Thus Belichick maintained an aggressive passing attack even after his quarterback threw three picks because he knew passing, and putting the game in Brady's hands gave the Pats the best chance of winning. Schottenheimer, meanwhile, abandoned what had been a highly successful running attack—the very thing that had earned his team most of its 14 wins—the second the match became competitive (which is to say, when the Pats pulled into a tie with 4:30 remaining on the clock). And Belichick kept his veteran team focused on the game while Schottenheimer stood by and watched his young players launch into a victory celebration as soon as they went ahead 21–13 with most of nine minutes remaining to play.

So Belichick coached circles around his rival in that playoff game. That was expected.

And so was Brady's level-headedness in the face of adversity. Brady, who had thrown only five interceptions during 12 previous playoff games, put the ball in San Diego's hands three times that day. But on the biggest pass play of the game, a third-and-10 at the New England 34 with less than three minutes remaining, Brady stayed cool in the face of a San Diego blitz and found wide receiver Reche Caldwell 49 yards downfield on the right sideline.

That set up Stephen Gostkowski's 31-yard field goal that put the winning points on the board with a little over one minute left.

But, like great coaching from Belichick, great play in the clutch by Brady is only what Pats fans expect.

What no one could have expected was the play in which Troy Brown, without a nanosecond's delay or hesitation, made the switch from wide receiver to defensive back and saved the game.

On a fourth-and-five at the San Diego 41 with the Pats down by eight with 6:25 to play, Brady spotted Brown open 10 yards away in the middle of the field and let fly. But safety Marlon McCree had a great read on the play and got to the ball first, making the pick.

Had McCree had the presence of mind not to catch the fourth-down pass but simply to slap the ball to the ground, or if he'd gone down and ended the play after making the interception, the Chargers likely would have been able to run out most of the clock, all but clinching a victory. He didn't.

McCree chose to showboat. But as the safety looked for a lane to the Patriots' end zone, Brown snuck back into the play. The veteran wide receiver, who'd spent much of the season lining up as an extra defensive back as injuries took their toll on the Patriots' secondary, switched gears, ran in behind McCree, and stripped the ball from the safety's hands. Caldwell recovered the fumble, giving the Pats a new set of downs.

And, of course, Brady and the offense turned the opportunity into a touchdown and a two-point conversion that tied the score.

That doesn't happen most of the time. What does happen is that the interception goes for a touchdown that puts the home team ahead by 15. Or someone makes a tackle downfield and the home team grinds out the clock before going up by 11 or 15. And the visitors go home to start preparing for their next game—in September.

But that's one of the reasons you put Troy Brown on the field to begin with.

"He wasn't just a receiver on that play, he was a football player," defensive end Richard Seymour said after the game. "Troy always comes up with plays like that. If there's one guy I look up to, it's Troy Brown."

NO, THEY CAN'T: DYING IN THE RCA DOME

The game was over by halftime. Peyton Manning and the Indianapolis Colts were done, beaten once again by Tom Brady and the New England Patriots. It was just a matter of running 30 minutes off the clock and booking air passage to Miami for Super Bowl XLI.

That's how it seemed, anyhow.

And there was no reason it should have seemed otherwise.

The Pats were ahead 21–6. The Colts had kicked their second field goal of the game just before the end of the half, but that didn't matter. The Colts weren't even getting back into that game, never mind winning it. Because losing to the Patriots in the play-offs had become one of the things that made the Colts the Colts. Choking at home in the postseason was another.

The thing that made the Patriots the Patriots? Easy. They had won in the playoffs 12 times in 13 trips since Brady became New England's starting quarterback. And that included a spectacular comeback victory over the San Diego Chargers, the AFC's top-seeded team, just a week earlier. It was January and the Pats were on a roll. Again.

Besides, as always, the breaks were going the Patriots' way. On their second drive of the game, with the score still 0–0, the Pats had driven to the Colts' 4-yard line, when on third-and-one a botched exchange from Brady to running back Laurence Maroney put the ball on the ground. But after the ball bounced into the end zone, left guard Logan Mankins fell on it, putting the Pats ahead by a touchdown.

Then five minutes into the second quarter, cornerback Asante Samuel jumped wide receiver Marvin Harrison's route, snatched a Manning pass out of the air, and bolted 39 yards for a touchdown.

With a Corey Dillon touchdown run and a field goal by Adam Vinatieri (now playing for the Colts) in between, Samuel's pick six made the score 21–3. That should have been more than enough.

And so at halftime it appeared that the naysayers would be proven wrong.

The fans and experts who had spent the entire 2006 season doubting New England's ability to succeed with a patchwork corps of receivers were being shown that with this team, this coach, this quarterback, it didn't matter who was catching the ball. They were learning that the Pats didn't need Deion Branch, the Super Bowl XXXIX MVP who led the team with 78 catches for 998 yards in 2006. Branch, whose contract dispute in the off-season had ended with a trade to Seattle on September 11, was no different than David Givens, who'd bolted for New Orleans in free agency a year earlier after two stellar seasons in New England. Or David Patten. Or anybody except Troy Brown, the soul of the team.

Branch had been a cog in an offensive machine masterfully engineered by Bill Belichick and operated with maximum efficiency

TROY BROWN, PART TIME DB

Kick returner, wide receiver, defensive back—Troy Brown is a Patriots legend because he's done everything he's been asked to do (including once lining up at quarterback in a preseason game) and done it well. Brown, who saw some action as a DB during the 2004 season, made regular appearances as a nickel back in 2006 when injuries thinned out the Pats' secondary. Brown made 17 tackles, broke up five passes, and picked off three balls in 2006.

by Brady. The quarterback threw passes to whomever was open, and they caught them. Wide receiver, tight end, tailback, *linebacker*. It didn't matter.

So, sure, the acquisition of Doug Gabriel in a trade with the Oakland Raiders hadn't worked out in the end (Gabriel was waived and back in a Raiders uniform by mid-December). But the other new receivers were working out fine. Free agent Reche Caldwell, who'd come over from San Diego in the off-season, led the Pats with 61 catches for 760 yards during the regular season. He caught seven passes for 80 yards in the divisional round game against his former team. And Jabar Gaffney, an early October signing who had spent four seasons in Houston and training camp in Philadelphia, pulled down 11 balls for 142 yards in six regular season starts. Then he came on like crazy in the playoffs, snagging eight catches for 104 yards against the New York Jets in the wild-card round and 10 for 103 against San Diego a week later.

With every pass Caldwell and Gaffney caught, Branch's departure seemed less meaningful.

Plus, Brown, tight end Benjamin Watson, and veteran tailback Kevin Faulk were always there for Brady to fall back on.

On top of that, there were Dillon, Maroney, and Faulk, whom Belichick said made up the best group of running backs he'd ever coached. The trio of backs had amassed 1,680 yards on the ground that season and most of another 700 through the air (with Faulk accounting for 356 of them).

The Pats also had a defense that ranked second in the league in points allowed during the regular season, allowing less than 15 points a game on average. They'd given up 37 points in their first two playoff games but 21 of those had come in an away game with the Chargers, who had the highest scoring offense in the league.

That the Colts had the second-highest scoring offense in the NFL certainly didn't seem to matter at the half.

The Patriots were 2–0 against the Colts in the postseason since the rivalry between the teams had been revived in the Belichick/Brady-Tony Dungy/Manning era. Indianapolis had managed to take two straight regular season games against New England (after losing the previous four), but this wasn't the regular season.

Neither was it the first time the Patriots had been forced to go on the road in pursuit of the AFC crown. They'd done it successfully in Pittsburgh five years earlier.

Nor was it the first time the Colts had collapsed at home in a big playoff game. A year earlier, having entered the postseason as the conference's top seed, they'd fallen to the Steelers in Indianapolis in the divisional round.

It was just the way things went. The Colts got all the love during the regular season only to fall in the playoffs. And the Patriots, whatever they were up against, just found ways to win postseason games.

The only thing that wasn't really humming for New England in the first half was the passing game. And even that wasn't exactly terrible. Brady had connected on eight of 12 passes for 91 yards. Those numbers seemed bound to improve dramatically in the second half as Indy's defensive backs and pass rushers wore down.

It was really just a matter of getting to the point where Belichick could begin game planning for the Chicago Bears.

And it didn't seem like too big a deal that the Colts mounted a 76-yard scoring drive on their first possession of the third quarter. Indianapolis was destined to score seven at some point during the game. The score was still 21–13. And the Pats offense hadn't yet touched the ball in the second half.

Then they did. They went three and out.

The Colts took possession at their 24-yard line for the second time in the half and again marched down the field with relative ease. Late in the drive Indianapolis got some help from the officials by way of a phantom pass interference call on Pats cornerback Ellis Hobbs in the end zone (a call so bad the NFL, which almost never admits officials make mistakes, later wrote a letter of apology to Hobbs). That changed what should have been a third-and-seven at the New England 19-yard line to a first-and-goal at the 1-yard line. Two snaps later, the Colts had scored a touchdown and a two-point conversion to tie the game.

Eleven minutes into the second half the Patriots' trip to Super Bowl XLI had been put on hold.

The teams traded touchdowns on their next possessions, moving the score to 28–28. Caldwell dropped what should have been an easy touchdown pass during the Pats' scoring drive, but the mistake was rendered meaningless when Gaffney capitalized on his scoring opportunity one play later.

Trouble was, that drop wouldn't be Caldwell's last of the game. And his next one would prove far more costly.

On third-and-seven at the Colts' 10-yard line with just under eight minutes remaining in the game, Caldwell lined up right and found himself uncovered. He had a short, clear path to the end zone ahead of him as Brady took the snap and fired his way. The pass was perfect. The catch was nonexistent.

The Patriots had to settle for a field goal, which the Colts matched on their next possession. And the four points Caldwell's drop left off the scoreboard would prove the Pats' undoing.

The Pats were able to go ahead 34–31 with another field goal. But when the Colts capped an 80-yard drive with a three-yard Joseph Addai touchdown run late in the fourth quarter, instead of tying the contest, they moved ahead 38–34. With a minute remaining, that put the Pats in an almost impossible situation. There was no seeing if they could get into field goal range and once again pull off a huge win at the end of regulation. There was no knowing they'd at least have a chance to win it in overtime.

It was do or die. And now the breaks were going Indy's way. They had been throughout the second half, starting with the call against Hobbs, moving on to the early fourth quarter play in which center Jeff Saturday scored a touchdown by falling on a ball that had been dropped at the goal line by running back Dominic Rhodes, then on to Caldwell's costly blunder.

So when Colts cornerback Marlin Jackson stepped in front of Watson and picked off Brady at the Colts' 35-yard line with 16 seconds left on the clock, there was no Troy Brown strip to save the game. There was no pass interference call somewhere away from the play to give the Patriots another chance.

And there was no fourth trip to the Super Bowl in six years in the offing for New England. There was just a kneel-down by Manning and a victory celebration by the home team and its fans.

Eight months later there was no Reche Caldwell in a Patriots uniform either. Jabar Gaffney survived the off-season (and demonstrated why with key catches scattered through the 2007 campaign), but Caldwell, having proved the naysayers right, was replaced by Randy Moss, Wes Welker, and Donté Stallworth, the building blocks of the greatest offense in NFL history.

In professional sports, disappointment, like elation, often proves to be short-lived.

GOOD CALLS, BAD CALLS (YOU KNOW THEY'VE HAD THEIR SHARE)

WHAT ROUGHING? THE WORST POSSIBLE CALL AT THE WORST POSSIBLE TIME

Maybe it's a function of New England's collective Irish memory. Or maybe it's simply true that some wrongs can never be put right.

Whatever the reason, there's just no uttering the name Ben Dreith in the presence of a longtime Patriots fan without eliciting a groan, a curse, or maybe even the expression of some disturbing, violent fantasy. Not even after 32 years and three Super Bowl championships.

Suggesting that a fan take some historical perspective and forget what Dreith did to the Patriots on December 18, 1976, would be like telling Red Sox fans to concentrate on the team's two recent World Series championships and let go of their two-decades-old grudge against Bill Buckner. Yeah, you might be making what amounts to a call to reason. And letting go might be both psychologically sound and spiritually uplifting. But there's no chance of it happening. Not ever.

So what exactly did Dreith do to earn the eternal enmity of Patriots fans?

The answer depends on who's asked the question.

If you were to ask Dreith, he'd tell you, as he always has, that he made a perfectly reasonable roughing the passer call on Patriots defensive tackle Ray "Sugar Bear" Hamilton. Dreith swears he saw Hamilton intentionally swat Oakland Raiders quarterback

GIVING HIM THE BUSINESS

Although his name is infamous in New England, Ben Dreith is more widely known for a call he made against New York Jets tackle Marty Lyons in a 1986 game against the Buffalo Bills. Lyons had taken a few shots at Bills quarterback Jim Kelly's head after a tackle, drawing a flag for unsportsman-like conduct. "We have a personal foul on number 99 [mistaking Lyons for Mark Gastineau] of the defense," Dreith announced. "After he tackled the quarterback, he's giving him the business down there."

Ken Stabler's helmet after tipping a pass late in the fourth quarter of a first-round playoff game.

The Pats were up 21–17 at the time, and they almost certainly would have finished the Raiders off had Dreith not thrown his flag. The penalty came after Stabler's pass bounced off Hamilton's fingertips and flipped toward the sideline incomplete. Had the play stood, the Raiders would have faced fourth-and-18 and almost certain doom. Instead they got a new set of downs and the momentum to pull off a last-second win.

When *The Boston Globe* tracked down Dreith 25 years later—strangely enough, on the eve of the January 2002 Pats-Raiders playoff game that would include the now-famous tuck call—he was still sticking by his story. "You bet," he said. "Roughing the passer. He got a piece of the ball, but he gave Stabler kind of a karate chop on the side of the head on the way down."

That's one man's interpretation. And at the time Dreith was the one man whose opinion counted.

Ask a Raiders fan what happened and you might get a strong defense of Dreith's call. Or you might get a sly snicker or a half smile and a shrug. Oakland went on to win Super Bowl XI that year, and when you're a fan of any team you take the big wins by hook or by crook if that's how they come.

Turn to an objective source and you'll hear that Dreith blew it. Hamilton's hand did graze Stabler's helmet but only barely. In today's NFL, with its emphasis on protecting quarterbacks and preventing head injuries, the play would almost certainly draw a flag. But in 1976 such calls were unheard of. In those days players actually had to take a shot at a quarterback to elicit a roughing call. And all it takes is a brief look at the play to recognize that Hamilton wasn't trying to hit Stabler with a karate chop or anything else.

When ESPN.com's Page 2 compiled a list of the 10 "Worst Calls in Sports History" in 2001, it gave the penalty on Hamilton a dishonorable mention.

Bring a longtime Patriots fan—or, hell, the child of a longtime Patriots fan—into the conversation, and you'll get something else entirely. You might hear that Dreith made the worst call in professional sports history, a call that delayed New England's first trip to the Super Bowl by nine years and robbed one of the best squads in team history of its due. Or you might hear that Dreith was the head of an officiating crew that conspired to make sure Oakland advanced in the playoffs.

That latter contention, in reality, is more than a bit of a stretch. There's a "fix-was-in" mentality that almost invariably rises among some fans whenever a game turns on one or more bad calls. (There are those Pats fans even now who believe the erroneous pass interference call against Ellis Hobbs in the 2006–07 AFC Championship is evidence that the league wanted Peyton Manning, Tony Dungy, and the Indianapolis Colts to finally win a Super Bowl. And there are Raiders fans who believe the tuck call in the 2001–02 divisional round game at New England proves the NFL wanted the *Patriots* to prevail in the first postseason since September 11.) But like most conspiracy theories, loaded game scenarios typically turn on plots far too complex to actually carry out, particularly in a sport given to odd bounces of its oblong ball.

That said, it's not as if Dreith's call against Hamilton was the only questionable bit of officiating that took place in Oakland that afternoon.

Early on, Raiders safety George Atkinson delivered a forearm blow to Patriots tight end Russ Francis that broke Francis's nose. (Atkinson would later explain, "I just wanted to show him how it was going to be.") Even in that sometimes brutal era, the shot

SHOULDA, COULDA, WOULDA

If winning weren't everything, the 1976 Patriots would be considered along-side the 2007, 2004, and 2003 squads as among the best ever fielded in New England. The team was stacked with talent—including future Hall of Fame players John Hannah and Mike Haynes—and paid it off, beating its opponents by an average of 10 points per game. That average falls behind only the 2004 team, which topped opponents by an average of 11 points, and the 2007 squad (featuring the best offense in league history) that managed a ridiculous point differential of close to 20 per game. Had the '76 team been able to play out its potential, it's likely the '07 squad would have gone into Super Bowl XLII in pursuit of "one for the thumb."

defined unnecessary roughness. But although the infraction took place in front of an official, no flag was thrown.

Phantom holding calls were made on the Pats throughout the game, more than one of them negating significant gains. But when Francis was mugged by Raiders linebacker Phil Villapiano on third-and-six at the Oakland 33 late in the fourth quarter, again with an official standing right there, no yellow flag was ever produced.

And it was that noncall, really, that set up the bogus penalty on Hamilton.

The Pats could have run the clock down to next to no time before scoring a touchdown or at least a field goal, had the inter-ference against Francis drawn a flag, or had Francis not been interfered with to begin with (Villapiano admitted years later that he held Francis because he knew the other option was to surren-der a first down). Instead New England was left to try a 50-yard field goal, which failed, setting up Oakland's final drive.

Shortly thereafter, with the Raiders trailing by four points and less than a minute to play, Oakland lined up on third-and-18 at the Patriots 28. Stabler dropped back to pass and Hamilton, coming hard across the line, put his hand up and deflected the ball. The game was all but over. The Raiders would have to go for it on fourth-and-18, and there was no way that was working out for them. But Dreith threw the flag, giving Oakland a first down. The Raiders advanced to the 1-yard line, and then Stabler ran the ball into the end zone with 10 seconds remaining.

It wasn't just a matter of the call costing the Patriots a victory, though. That game marked the team's first postseason appearance since its crushing defeat by San Diego in the 1963 AFL Championship. It should have ended in vindication.

What's more, the path from Oakland to the Super Bowl was clear.

The Pittsburgh Steelers, whom the Raiders ended up destroying in the AFC Championship, were banged up badly and not going anywhere. And it was a given going into the postseason that the NFC representative, which turned out to be the Minnesota Vikings, would be losing the Super Bowl to the team from the much stronger AFC.

The 1976 Raiders were a great football team. They lost only one game in the regular season. But that one loss was a doozy: a 48–17 blowout at the hands of the Patriots in Schaefer Stadium.

The Pats, who finished the season 11–3, were arguably a better team than the eventual champs. They outplayed Oakland in that playoff game, too.

But because of Ben Dreith, none of that mattered. And when you look at it that way, maybe there really is no forgiving—or forgetting—due.

THE RULES ARE THE RULES: THE TUCK

In the Subway commercial, the referee admits to making a bad call and promises, "I'll penalize the other team for no good reason in the second half to even things up."

In the real world, and specifically within the microcosm of the Patriots-Raiders rivalry, it took 25 years for the refs to even things up. And depending on how you look at things, they may not have done it yet.

What isn't in dispute is that without intervention from the officials, the Patriots almost certainly would have lost their

2001–02 divisional round playoff game against the visiting Raiders.

The Pats had clawed their way back from a 13–3 deficit at the start of the fourth quarter to trail the Raiders 13–10 as the game drew to a close. New England had moved the ball across midfield just before the two-minute warning. And with 1:50 remaining they lined up on first-and-10 at the Oakland 42-yard line.

Tom Brady, who'd been playing well in his first postseason start, dropped back to pass, when Raiders cornerback Charles Woodson came flying, unblocked, around the right side of the Patriots' line. Woodson laid a powerful hit on Brady that knocked the football out of the quarterback's hand. Oakland linebacker Greg Biekert was there to fall on the ball, recovering for Oakland and effectively sealing a narrow Raiders victory.

The game was over, and with it the Patriots' season. The next stop for Oakland was the AFC Championship game. The next stop for New England was training camp, with the near certainty of a quarterback controversy looming. (It would have been almost impossible for Bill Belichick to persuade the team to trade Drew Bledsoe, the superstar who was like a son to Robert Kraft, had the final meaningful play of the Pats' season featured Brady coughing up the ball at a critical moment.)

Then the officials in the replay booth called down to say they wanted to take another look at the fumble. What referee Walt Coleman decided he saw on the tape is still the subject of controversy.

Coleman concluded that Brady was in the process of tucking the ball under his arm following either a pump fake or an aborted pass attempt when Woodson hit him. According to NFL rules, such a tuck constitutes the final action in the continuing motion of an intended forward pass. That meant the play had resulted not in a fumble but an incompletion.

It was hard to grasp at the time, and it remains hard to swallow for Raiders fans because Brady clearly had no plan of throwing the football at the time Woodson hit him. But the rule is in the books and it was Coleman's job to enforce the rules as they're written. Incomplete pass.

The ball went back to the Patriots. And five plays later, Adam Vinatieri boomed a 45-yard kick through the driving snow, sending the game to overtime—in which the Patriots won.

Woodson was anything but shy about expressing his opinion on the reversal in his postgame press conference. "That's some bullshit," he said. "That's exactly how I feel. That was a bullshit call. It never should have been overturned. The guy pumped the ball, brung it back down. You know, maybe he wanted to bring it back up to throw it again, but I hit him before he had a chance to do that. Game over."

He wasn't alone. Other Raiders players expressed outrage. Raiders owner Al Davis expressed outrage. And the costumed denizens of Raider Nation collectively freaked out. While the game is known in New England, and most of America, as the Snow Bowl, in and around Oakland, California, it's still called the Snow Job.

The Raiders faithful continue to insist that the original call on the field was correct. Brady wasn't in the process of tucking the ball away, they claim. He had tucked it and was preparing to run when Woodson hit him and knocked the ball loose.

In Patriots country the call is largely viewed the other way. There's no question about whether Brady was engaged in a throwing movement as Woodson came around the corner and drew a bead on the quarterback. And if Brady finished his tuck before Woodson got to him, it was by a split second at best. If Coleman

THE TUCK RULE

Rule 3, Section 21, Article 2, Note 2, which was introduced to the NFL's official rules in 1999 states: "When a Team A player is holding the ball to pass it forward, any intentional forward movement of his hand starts a forward pass, even if the player loses possession of the ball as he is attempting to tuck it back toward his body. Also, if the player has tucked the ball into his body and then loses possession, it is a fumble."

put his head under the replay hood, took a close look and saw a tuck, then there was a tuck. The rules are the rules.

At any rate, if the call was off the mark it wasn't nearly so obviously bad as Ben Dreith's call on Hamilton had been 25 years earlier. So even for those few in the Pats' camp who suspect Coleman may have made the wrong call, there is a sense that what goes around comes around. If you have to live with the questionable calls that go against your team, everyone else has to live with the ones that go against theirs. Especially when the team that got the best of one call winds up on the other side of the next. That's called karma.

What's nearly impossible to do is to form an objective opinion on the call. From one angle it appears Brady couldn't possibly have completed his throwing motion before Woodson reached him. So it was a tuck. From another, it seems Brady has the ball put away. So it was a fumble. Every angle, however, is obscured by other players and by the fast-falling snow that impaired visibility on the field and through the camera lens throughout the game.

If Oakland supporters have a solid argument, it's that there's not enough evidence in the video for Coleman to have overturned the call on the field properly. By rule, a call can only be reversed by replay if the video offers conclusive evidence that the original ruling was incorrect.

Conclusive evidence, though, is in the eye of the beholder. The reversal was made. And Mike Pereira, the NFL's vice president of officiating, has consistently stated that Coleman made the right call.

Most importantly, though, the tuck call is unlike Dreith's roughing penalty in that it didn't effectively decide the game. While Oakland would certainly have held on for the win had the fumble ruling been confirmed, the Raiders had more than ample opportunity to secure their victory even after the Pats got the ball back. And unlike the roughing call on Hamilton, the tuck ruling didn't advance the ball for the Patriots or result in a fresh set of downs. New England still faced second and 10 at the Oakland 42. And the snow was still falling hard.

If the Raiders had managed to prevent Brady's 13-yard completion on the next play, the Pats might never have advanced far enough for Vinatieri to kick the tying field goal.

And yes, that's *tying* field goal. The Pats didn't win the game on the drive the tuck call kept alive. They had to do that in overtime. Oakland had plenty of chances to step up during New England's 15-play, eight-and-a-half-minute scoring drive in the extra period. They didn't. And all their complaining about it after the fact hasn't changed that any more than it changed the final score.

THERE'S NO SUCH THING AS FACE GUARDING

Phil Simms announced that Ellis Hobbs had been flagged for face guarding.

And it sounded reasonable for a second, partially because it was coming from the one of the best game analysts on TV. Simms was in the booth for the 2006–07 AFC Championship game between the Patriots and the Indianapolis Colts because he was the network's top guy. So when he explained the call against the Pats' second-year cornerback, you might have figured you could take his word for it. You'd have figured wrong.

Hobbs had just made what looked like a spectacular defensive play. He had prevented Reggie Wayne from making a 19-yard touchdown catch, leaping in front of the Indy wideout just as Peyton Manning's pass arrived and knocking the ball down with the back of his left biceps.

Down 21–13 in the third quarter, the Colts would have one more chance to pick up seven yards, this time with the Pats D fairly certain it wouldn't have to worry about a run. If the Patriots could hold Indy to short yards or no yards on third down, they'd probably be able to preserve their lead.

Then the flags flew. Referee Bill Carollo announced the call: pass interference on Hobbs. The Colts would get a first-and-goal at the 1-yard line.

"Face guarding," Simms announced. "Ellis Hobbs jumps up, just tries to get in the way of Reggie Wayne. Does not see the football. Does not play it. Easy call."

Patriots cornerback Ellis Hobbs outruns Indianapolis Colts defenders Matt Giordano (43), Dexter Reid (36), and Freddy Keiaho (54) on an 80-yard kickoff return in the third quarter of the AFC Championship Game on January 21, 2007, in Indianapolis.

Easy indeed. If only face guarding were illegal.

The rules regarding what constitutes defensive pass interference in the NFL are anything but simple. The same goes for enforcement of those rules. So interference calls can at times be highly subjective. Was a defender attempting to make a play on the ball or was he simply cutting off the receiver's route? Was the pass catchable? Was the contact incidental? Was the ball tipped before contact took place? Officials routinely have to answer those questions, among others, in the seconds between watching a play take place and deciding whether to throw a flag.

What isn't subjective is this: if there's no contact, there's no interference. Ever. Face guarding may sound official and somehow real, but it isn't. A defender can block a receiver's view all day long, and if the officials are calling the game right he'll never draw a flag until he puts a hand on his guy.

That's the trouble with the call on Hobbs. Looking at the replay it was clear that Hobbs had never come into contact with Wayne. Simms saw that fact, saw a flag on the ground, heard a penalty announced, and drew a quick conclusion.

Simms's confusion probably also had to do with how the rules work when there is contact. A defensive back who is trying to make a play on the ball and comes in contact with a receiver as a result hasn't committed interference. Thus a DB who bumps his man without looking back over his shoulder for the ball is almost always called for a penalty. A DB who does look for the ball is called only if he grabs the receiver or otherwise prevents him from trying to make a play.

Chances are, Simms simply added the looking for the ball standard to the fact that there had been no contact and came up with face guarding.

There was no official call of face guarding—the call on the field was plain old pass interference—but Simms's statement created a lasting impression that Hobbs had committed the phantom infraction. To this day there are fans in New England and Indianapolis who will say Hobbs was called for face guarding.

Of course, what people think mostly adds up to nothing. What matters is what happened. And what happened was that Hobbs was called, and the Patriots were hit with a costly penalty when no infraction of any kind had taken place.

All Ellis Hobbs did was play smart football.

Although Wayne had managed to get by Hobbs briefly at the beginning of the play, the hardworking cornerback never gave up on his man. He pulled back up close to Wayne in the end zone and when he saw the receiver's eyes widen, betraying the approach of the ball, he jumped off the ground as high as he could, arms stretched out above his head in hopes of disrupting Wayne's sight and preventing a catch. Having the ball bounce off his arm was something Hobbs couldn't count on, but it kept the ball out of Wayne's hands just the same.

Hobbs had done his job.

IT'S TOO LATE TO SAY YOU'RE SORRY

While there may be a question about what the interference penalty against Ellis Hobbs in the 2006–07 AFC Championship meant to the outcome of the game, there's none regarding whether the call was correct. The NFL, which almost never admits that officials have blown a call, later conceded that Hobbs had not interfered with Colts receiver Reggie Wayne. The league sent a letter of apology to Hobbs in the off-season. Hobbs took the letter, but told the *Boston Herald*, "It's a little late for that now." He was right. The AFC Championship was a memory. And Super Bowl XLI had already been played.

But instead of third-and-seven at the 19, a very defensible down for the Patriots' stout red zone defense, the Colts faced first-and-goal at the 1.

That inarguably made a difference in the game.

Two snaps later the Colts had tied the score.

And while it would be just plain silly to argue that the conference championship turned on the bad call—the Patriots, who led 21–6 at halftime, had the entire second half to put the Colts away and failed repeatedly to do it—there's no pretending its effects weren't felt.

Had the Colts had been forced to settle for a field goal on that drive, they would have come away still trailing by five. And the touchdown the Patriots scored on their next possession would have made the difference 12. (There's always the possibility that the Colts might have gone for it on fourth down, of course, but it's too remote to consider.)

It's impossible to say how Indy would have handled trailing by two scores after three quarters. (Would they have gone for it on fourth-and-three from the Pats' 18 midway through the final period rather than kicking a field goal?) But even if most of the rest of the game had gone exactly as it did, the Colts would have had to turn a two-point conversion after Joseph Addai's late touchdown just to pull into a tie.

What can be said with relative certainty is that the winner of the AFC Championship that January 21 was going on to win Super Bowl XLI. The Chicago Bears might have been monsters when they took on NFC opponents, but they didn't have anything like the stuff to beat the Pats or the Colts. (Consider the fact that Indianapolis played poorly in the Super Bowl and still came out on top 29–17.)

Still, the fact that the Patriots didn't get the opportunity to face the Bears was their own fault. They played poorly enough to blow a giant halftime lead. The refs didn't do that to New England. The Patriots did it to themselves.

So the Patriots went home after the game and never uttered a word of complaint about the call. Hobbs defended himself when asked about the play—"I didn't touch him," he insisted. "That's all I'm going to say, because I don't want to get fined." But the team stayed mum.

And then Bill Belichick and Scott Pioli spent the off-season building a team that would never again have to wonder what might have been if the refs hadn't blown one call.

INS AND OUTS

TWO STOPS TO CANTON, PART ONE: NICK BUONICONTI

There may come a time two or three decades from now when the list of one-time Patriots enshrined in the Pro Football Hall of Fame stretches out the way the lists for the Chicago Bears and Green Bay Packers do now. Given the Patriots teams that have taken the field over the past eight seasons, it's certain the list will grow.

For the moment, though, there are precisely four players in the Hall of Fame who spent time with the Pats. There's John Hannah, the career Patriot whose dominance during his 13 years on New England's offensive line won him a place in Canton in his first year of eligibility. There's linebacker Andre Tippett, whose election in 2008 made him the only other career Patriot in the Hall of Fame. And then there are Nick Buoniconti and Mike Haynes, players more closely associated with other teams—the Miami Dolphins and the Los Angeles Raiders—than the squad they started their careers with.

Buoniconti in particular is virtually never associated with the Pats by anyone from outside of New England. Not only is Buoniconti thought of as a Dolphin through-and-through, but he's also been one of the more visible ex-Fins through the years, particularly during his 21-year stint as cohost of HBO's *Inside the NFL*.

When the 2007 Patriots made their run at becoming only the second team to complete a season without suffering a loss, the press sought out Buoniconti as a representative of the undefeated 1972 Dolphins, rarely mentioning the fact that he's also a member of the Patriots Hall of Fame.

It stands to reason that Buoniconti would be remembered as a Dolphins player.

Sure, Buoniconti was drafted by the Pats in 1962 and played seven seasons in Boston before he was traded to Miami. And sure, the Springfield, Massachusetts, native had a good deal of individual success with the Patriots, making 17 sacks, picking off 24 passes, and going to the AFL All-Star game five times.

But the AFL wasn't a high-visibility league, and the Patriots were anything but a spotlight team. The biggest splash Boston made during Buoniconti's tenure was in their trip to the 1963 AFL Championship, where they were throttled 51–10 by the San Diego Chargers.

Patriots linebacker Nick Buoniconti, seen here in August 1967, is one of only four Patriots enshrined in the Pro Football Hall of Fame, though he is generally remembered for his post-Pats playing days with the Miami Dolphins.

As with other members of the AFL-era Patriots—players like Babe Parilli, Gino Cappelletti, and Jim Nance—it really didn't matter that Buoniconti brought a lot to the game. It's not that others got the glory; it was simply that there wasn't a lot of glory to go around.

When Buoniconti arrived in Miami, on the other hand, there was glory in abundance just around the corner. The Super Bowl era had begun. The Dolphins were building toward greatness. And although the unit Buoniconti would lead was labeled the "No-Name Defense," its players were anything but anonymous, just less recognized than the members of Miami's high-flying offense.

Buoniconti continued to realize personal success, going to a sixth AFL All-Star game and, after the merger, to a pair of Pro Bowls. He was the Dolphins' MVP in 1969, 1970, and 1973.

More important than all that, though, Buoniconti's football smarts and on-field leadership played a significant role in getting the Fins to Super Bowls VI, VII, and VIII, the latter two of which Miami won.

So, yeah, Buoniconti is a Dolphin for good reason.

COULD HAVE DONE WORSE

The Patriots never got much production out of Jim Plunkett, the Heisman-winning quarterback they took with the first overall pick in the 1971 draft. But at least they got some value for him in the end. The Pats traded Plunkett to San Francisco in 1976, receiving two first-round picks in the '76 draft, as well as first- and second-rounders in 1977. They used those selections to bring in:

- Pete Brock, who gave the Pats 12 seasons as a center and guard.
- Tim Fox, whose six seasons at safety included a Pro Bowl year (1980).
- Raymond Clayborn, who picked off 36 balls and went to three Pro Bowls during his 13 seasons as a Patriot.
- Horace Ivory, a capable running back and outstanding kick returner who lasted five seasons.

Still, he might never have become a professional football player at all had it not been for the Boston Patriots.

The Pats took a chance on Buoniconti in the 13th round of the 1962 AFL draft despite the fact that he was widely considered too small to succeed in the pros. Buoniconti had been a standout player at Notre Dame, but at 5'9", 210 pounds, he failed to impress pro scouts. And after Fighting Irish coach Joe Kuharich refused to recommend his team captain to NFL scouts, claiming he feared for Buoniconti's safety, every team in the established league took a pass.

It took 102 picks before Boston saw fit to give Buoniconti a try in the new league. But the move paid off immediately. Buoniconti was named Patriots Rookie of the Year in 1962. And he quickly gained a reputation for being the most driven player on the field—and the most dangerous.

Buoniconti was the model of the versatile, unpredictable middle linebacker. He could show up virtually anywhere on the field, charging through the line on a blitz here, dropping into coverage there. And when he showed up near the ball, he usually flattened someone. Buoniconti might have been on the small side for a pro linebacker, but he more than made up for his size with intensity and propensity for hitting harder than the bigger players.

It was Buoniconti's leadership abilities that would eventually punch his ticket out of town. Buoniconti became the team's player rep, which put him on the bad side of team owner Billy Sullivan, a man who never cared for organized labor. After the 1968 season, Sullivan shipped Buoniconti to the Dolphins for linebacker John Bramlett, quarterback Kim Hammond, and a fifth-round draft choice. Bramlett lasted two seasons, Hammond one (during which time Hammond appeared in all of three games, never starting once). And the Pats spent the draft choice on a new Notre Dame linebacker, Bob Olson, who never even made the team.

It would be almost 40 years before the Patriots would come out on the good side of such an uneven trade with the Dolphins.

Buoniconti, meanwhile, played six full and highly productive seasons in Miami. He'd slowed down a bit. But he hadn't lost anything in terms of intensity. And it was what Buoniconti delivered on the field for the Dolphins, in large part, that secured his admission to Canton in 2001.

TWO STOPS TO CANTON, PART TWO: MIKE HAYNES

The events that led to the Patriots trading star cornerback Mike Haynes to the Los Angeles Raiders midway through the 1983 season weren't all the team's fault. In some ways the culture and the business structure of the NFL in the early 1980s can be blamed for what happened.

Then again, the Sullivan family's unwavering cheapness also had more than a bit to do with it. By the time things fell apart with Haynes—in the form of a contract dispute that led the cornerback to sit out New England's first six games in '83—the Sullivans already had shipped safety Tim Fox and tight end Russ Francis to San Diego and San Francisco in order to save a buck.

But with all due respect to Fox and Francis (both fine football players who made significant contributions to the Patriots), losing those players was one thing; losing Mike Haynes was another.

Haynes was one of the best defensive backs in the league from the moment he arrived in Foxborough as the fifth overall selection in the 1976 draft. It helped that the team Haynes joined was loaded with talent on both sides of the ball. But the Patriots didn't make the young cornerback a star. Haynes became a standout player in the NFL for the same reasons he'd been one of the best players in Arizona State University history: he was fast, he was athletic, and he had great instincts for the ball.

At ASU Haynes had been known by the nickname "Luxury." "We just assign him to cover the opposition's best receiver and never give him any help, and the rest of our guys just go about their business," Sun Devils coach Frank Kush once explained. "He's luxury."

In Foxborough, Haynes was more of a necessity. Along with fellow rookie Fox (who had been taken with one of the first-round picks the Pats acquired from San Francisco in exchange for quarterback Jim Plunkett), Haynes helped turn a defense that had surrendered nearly 26 points a game in 1975 into one that allowed less than 17 a game in 1976. That turnaround played a major role in getting the Patriots into the playoffs for the first time in 13 years.

Haynes was a force in the secondary from the get-go, picking off eight balls in his rookie year, seven of them during a four-game stretch in November.

"That kid is a hell of a player," Joe Namath said following a November 21 game in which Haynes intercepted three passes. "He has great range. I didn't think I made any bad throws, and I was reading the coverages pretty well. He just went out there and got the ball."

In addition to his contributions on defense, Haynes returned 45 punts for an AFC-best 608 yards that season. His punt returns included touchdowns of 89 and 62 yards.

Haynes was named AFC Rookie of the Year and NFL Defensive Rookie of the Year, and he went to the first of what would be five straight Pro Bowls.

Haynes continued to make an impact even during the lean years that followed coach Chuck Fairbanks's departure in 1978. He qualified for the Pro Bowl in every season except 1981, when he missed half the season due to a collapsed lung. He led the team in interceptions for three straight years and recorded a total of 28 picks during his seven seasons.

IF IT DIDN'T WORK FOR MIKE HAYNES...

Wide receiver Deion Branch was probably as good as gone the minute he started insisting that the Pats renegotiate his deal prior to the 2006 season. The Super Bowl XXXIX MVP, who still had a year left on his rookie contract, wanted $40 million over six years. The Patriots were willing to give him $20 million over four. So Branch held out. And on September 11, 2006, he was shipped off to the Seattle Seahawks for a first-round pick, which the Pats used to bring in safety Brandon Merriweather.

As the start of the '83 season approached, however, Haynes was without a contract. And it became clear that Haynes and the team were not going to be able to reach a deal. The Pats played hardball with their best player—offering him just over $1 million on a three-year deal, which was approximately two-thirds of what he wanted—knowing Haynes' options were limited. In the years before free agency, players generally had three choices when contract talks reached a stalemate, none of them ideal: play for what the team that owned their rights offered, find another line of work, or hold out, sacrificing game checks in hopes of forcing the team to ante up or seek a trade.

Haynes went with option three, vowing he'd sit out the entire season before he'd play for less than he believed he was worth (incidentally, he was right about his value). He took the first six weeks of the season off while the Pats shopped for a deal and limped to a 2–4 record.

The Patriots finally found a trading partner in the Raiders on the day of the NFL trade deadline, striking a deal that would send Haynes to Los Angeles in exchange for a first-round pick in the 1984 draft and a second-rounder in 1985. (The Pats parlayed the '84 pick with their own to move up to the top of the draft and

HOW SOON CAN YOU LEAVE, TERRY GLENN?

Bill Parcells didn't like Terry Glenn when the Pats took him in the first round of the 1996 draft. (The coach felt Robert Kraft had crammed the Ohio State wide receiver down his throat—which he had.) Nobody liked Glenn by the time he left town in 2001. After a stellar rookie season, Glenn never again lived up to his potential. He was pouty and difficult and so roundly disliked that he was denied a ring after the Pats won Super Bowl XXXVI. Glenn went to Green Bay for two fourth-round picks in 2002. The Pats used the first of those to select outstanding defensive end Jarvis Green. They traded the second and a 2003 fifth-rounder to Denver so they could move up four spots and take Pro Bowl cornerback Asante Samuel.

grab wide receiver Irving Fryar. They used the '85 pick on safety Jim Bowman, who gave the team five entirely unspectacular seasons.)

As with virtually everything the Patriots touched in those days, however, the deal initially appeared to be cursed. NFL Commissioner Pete Rozelle disallowed the trade because it hadn't been officially registered until 15 minutes after the 4:00 PM, October 11 deadline. Raiders owner Al Davis jumped on the opportunity to sue his old nemesis Rozelle. And Haynes's lawyer, too, filed legal action in hopes of salvaging the trade.

Haynes, meanwhile, initiated talks with Donald Trump's USFL team, the New Jersey Generals, making it clear he was done with the Patriots regardless of how the various court cases turned out.

After the legal tussle went his way, Haynes reported to the Raiders in time to play during the last five weeks of the regular season and the playoffs. He recorded an interception in the Raiders' 38–9 victory over the Washington Redskins in Super Bowl XVIII.

In his seven seasons with Los Angeles, Haynes would go to three more Pro Bowls and record a total of 18 interceptions, one of which he returned for a touchdown. In 1984 he was awarded the George Halas Trophy, which recognizes outstanding defensive play.

Haynes was enshrined in the Pro Football Hall of Fame in 1997. Today he says he identifies himself as both a Patriot and a Raider. But in the minds of the football-watching public, he'll probably always be associated first with the team that put a ring on his finger.

THANKS FOR (SOME OF) THE MEMORIES: IRVING FRYAR

Irving Fryar was a mess. He was a mess before the Patriots made him the first overall pick in the 1984 draft. And he was a mess almost until the day Bill Parcells shipped him off to the Miami Dolphins.

Fryar got in trouble with drugs. He got in trouble with guns. He got into bar fights and car accidents. He took a baseball bat over the head outside a Providence nightclub. He got in a brawl with his wife and ended up taking six stitches in his hand days before one of the biggest games in Patriots history.

Fryar was the kind of guy current NFL commissioner Roger Goodell would have suspended for life sometime shortly after his second season.

And what made all of it hurt was that Fryar was an incredible talent on the field.

That's why New England traded their two first-round picks—their own and the one they'd received from the Los Angeles Raiders in exchange for Mike Haynes—to move up and make Fryar the first wide receiver in history selected first overall in the NFL draft.

Fryar had been an All-American in his senior year at the University of Nebraska, and he was recognized coming out of college as the best all-around athlete entering the NFL that year. The Pats had used their first-round pick the year before to bring in quarterback Tony Eason. They wanted to have someone special for Eason to throw to.

The Fryar the Patriots got was precisely the one they wanted. He practiced hard and played hard, kept himself in great condition, and did whatever his coaches asked of him. He was a talented receiver who not only never balked at throwing a block, but would knock defensive players over backward.

But he was also precisely what no team wants.

Four days before the 1985–86 AFC Championship game against Miami, Fryar fought with his wife, Jacqui. He knocked her down. She took a kitchen knife to his hand. He ended up in a cast and missed the game. (Though he did bounce back in time to catch the only Patriots touchdown in Super Bowl XX.)

When *The Boston Globe* reported on alleged widespread cocaine use by Patriots players in early 1986, Fryar's name was on the list of players who had reportedly tested positive for the drug.

Fryar left Sullivan Stadium without permission during a week 12 game against the Buffalo Bills in 1986 and crashed his car into a tree.

During the 1988 off-season, Fryar was stopped for speeding by a New Jersey state trooper. When the trooper walked up to Fryar's BMW, he spotted a hunting knife on the back seat and a holster

Irving Fryar, pictured here during his playing days with the Patriots, is remembered more for his problems with drugs, guns, and fighting than he is for his performance on the field. Photo courtesy of Getty Images.

on the floor. He searched the car and discovered a loaded shotgun and a handgun loaded with hollow-point bullets.

In 1989 Fryar was identified in Armen Keteyian's book *Big Red Confidential* as one of several players who allegedly used steroids while playing for Nebraska. The book also claimed Fryar and other Cornhuskers had received financial rewards for scoring touchdowns. Most damning, Keteyian claimed Fryar had intentionally dropped a pass in an effort to throw the 1984 Orange Bowl, which Nebraska lost to Miami.

And during a bye week in the middle of the 1990 season, Fryar was smashed in the head with a baseball bat outside a Providence nightclub and then arrested on a weapons charge. Fryar and another Pats receiver, Hart Lee Dykes, were leaving Club Shalimar just after 1:00 AM. when an argument with some other club-goers turned into a scuffle. Dykes was bashed in the face with a crutch, and Fryar was hit with the bat. Fryar then ran to his car, pulled out a gun, and pointed it at his assailants, who fled the scene. Dykes was hospitalized with an eye injury. Fryar was charged with carrying a gun without a permit.

Fryar got religion not long after that and has stayed out of trouble since.

Still, when Parcells showed up to remake the team in early 1993, making Fryar a *former* Patriot was one of his first orders of business. Fryar was shipped off to Miami for a pair of picks: a second-rounder the Pats used to get guard Todd Rucci, who spent seven seasons in New England, and a 1994 third-rounder with which they selected center Joe Burch, who didn't make the team.

Fryar more than salvaged his career after leaving the Patriots. He spent three seasons in Miami catching passes from Dan Marino, three more in Philadelphia, and two in Washington. A one-time Pro Bowler with the Patriots, Fryar went to two as a Dolphin and two more as an Eagle.

GOOD-BYE AND GOOD LUCK, PART ONE: DREW BLEDSOE
No one took great delight at seeing Drew Bledsoe leave Foxborough. Not even Tom Brady's earliest and biggest supporters.

Bledsoe might have been inconsistent on the field, but he was unquestionably a talented quarterback, not to mention a guy who played his heart out for the Patriots through his eight seasons as a starter (and again when the team called on him to sub for an injured Brady in the 2001–02 AFC Championship). He exhibited almost nothing but class during his time in New England. And while he was unhappy about losing his job to Brady as the result of an injury, no one outside the team knew it at the time because he had enough sense and enough character not to hurt his team by taking the matter public, a rarity in modern professional sports.

Bledsoe always drew cheers when he returned to Foxborough during his stint with the Buffalo Bills. It's unlikely any thoughtful or circumspect Pats fan took any measure of joy at seeing him once again lose his job to a young up-and-comer, this time Tony Romo, at the end of his career in Dallas.

And when Brady inevitably moves ahead of Bledsoe as the Patriots' all-time passing leader (likely sometime in the final four games of the 2008 season), there will almost certainly be those who think almost wistfully of Bledsoe and the hope he once represented.

Bledsoe did have to go following the 2001 season, though. There was no questioning that. Brady had taken over as New England's quarterback and leader. The Pats couldn't go back from that. They also couldn't keep Bledsoe around as a backup. There were cap implications inherent in trading a quarterback who had signed a 10-year, $103 million contract nine months before he lost his starting job, but there also would be cap implications involved in keeping a multimillion-dollar player around to stand on the sideline holding a clipboard.

Even if Bledsoe could have played effectively in Bill Belichick's offense, which he couldn't, his future was decided the moment the doctors cleared him to play and the coach elected to keep him on the bench.

Besides, Bledsoe had let the team know, if tacitly, that he wanted out. After Super Bowl XXXVI, he went home and stopped taking the Patriots' calls.

THE REST OF THE BEST OFF-SEASON EVER

The offensive makeover the Patriots engaged in during the 2007 off-season—at least partly in response to their collapse in the 2006–07 AFC Championship—didn't stop with the acquisition of Randy Moss and Wes Welker through trades. The Pats also imported free agent wideout Donté Stallworth, a five-year veteran of the New Orleans Saints and Philadelphia Eagles. Known as a dangerous runner after the catch, Stallworth pulled in 46 catches for 697 yards and three touchdowns. His athletic, 53-yard fingertip catch in the fourth quarter of the AFC divisional playoff game against Jacksonville set up the field goal that sealed the Pats' victory.

"It was clear to me he didn't want to be on this football team," Belichick told Michael Holley, author of *Patriot Reign.*

So the Patriots began entertaining offers. They attempted to make a deal before the 2002 draft but couldn't convince a team to agree to give up a first-round pick. Buffalo, the top suitor for Bledsoe's services, agreed on day two of the draft to send their 2003 first-rounder to the Pats in exchange for the quarterback.

During the '03 draft the Patriots packaged Buffalo's first-round pick with a sixth-round choice of their own to move up and take defensive end Ty Warren, who has become a key member of one of the best defensive lines in pro football. Having that extra first-round pick in '03 also made it possible for the Pats to trade away their own top pick that year for a package from Baltimore that included the Ravens' first pick in the 2004 draft. With that pick the Patriots took defensive tackle Vince Wilfork, whose play as a member of that same standout defensive front earned him a trip to the 2008 Pro Bowl.

Bledsoe left New England on a positive note. He took out a full-page ad in both of Boston's daily newspapers, using the space to publish an open letter thanking fans for their support.

"You demonstrated to me that I was more than a number on a field. I was a person you cared about," he wrote. "Please know that you have made a profound difference in my life and the way I will live it."

Bledsoe spent three seasons with the Bills, going to the Pro Bowl in 2002. He signed with Dallas as a free agent in 2005, reuniting with Parcells. He was released and opted to retire following the 2006 season.

Bledsoe never started a postseason game after leaving New England.

GOOD-BYE AND GOOD LUCK, PART TWO: ADAM VINATIERI

The Patriots never chose to part ways with the greatest place-kicker in team history. Adam Vinatieri chose to part ways with the Pats.

Just less than three weeks into the 2006 free agency period, Vinatieri signed a five-year, $12 million deal with the Indianapolis Colts (of all teams). He never gave the team that brought him into the NFL, and with which he won three Super Bowls, an opportunity to match the deal.

It's hard to say exactly why things happened that way, because Vinatieri won't. When asked, he's simply said that the Colts made him a good offer, and he didn't see any reason not to take it.

"When the Colts called, I told my agent, 'Let's not screw around,'" Vinatieri told *The Boston Globe* five months after he made the switch. "I told him, 'If Indy is interested, let's get this done.'"

It was clear from the start, though, that Vinatieri had been unhappy with the way the Patriots went about contract negotiations. Though he'd entered the league as an undrafted free agent, Vinatieri had gone well beyond proving his worth by the time his contract came up for renewal following the 2004 season.

He had come off a career year in which he was 31 for 33 on field goals and perfect on extra points. He had accounted for the winning points in two of the Patriots' Super Bowl victories (and the winning margin in all three). He wanted, and believed he deserved, a long-term deal.

He didn't get one. Instead the Patriots put the franchise tag on him, which gave him a guaranteed one-year salary of $2.5 million. Not a bad take-home, but not the kind of security any NFL player wants.

A year later the Patriots agreed not to franchise Vinatieri again. But neither did they show up at his door with the kind of deal they knew he wanted. So when the free agency period began March 3, Vinatieri started visiting teams.

The Colts hardly needed a visit. They'd seen plenty of Vinatieri over the years. And they'd seen more than enough of Mike Vanderjagt, a highly accurate kicker during the regular season with a bad habit of choking when his team needed him most (as he had in the Colts' AFC divisional playoff loss to Pittsburgh two months earlier).

In stark contrast to the hesitating Pats, the Colts couldn't write an offer to Vinatieri quickly enough.

Vinatieri said he understood that the Patriots viewed their business dealings with him unsympathetically. That's the team's model. So he took the same approach to free agency, going where the best offer was without feeling a need to give his original team a chance to make it work.

There was at least one other factor at work, though. Vinatieri's production had slipped some during the 2005 season. He hit only 20 of his 25 field-goal attempts. And at age 33 he wasn't likely to develop more leg. Not only did Vinatieri have to know he was probably negotiating his final deal, but he also can't have failed to consider the fact that kicking in an indoor environment is easier than kicking outside. Vinatieri had never missed a kick in Indy's RCA Dome. He was 39 of 43 kicking indoors over his career.

Chances are, Vinatieri recognized that his odds of extending his career would improve greatly with a change in work environment.

Whatever he did or didn't consider, though, the outcome was that the Pats' clutch kicker not only walked away, but walked straight to the team's biggest rival. That stung.

Vinatieri's move paid off in at least one regard. One season after he signed with the Colts, the kicker was the only member of the Patriots' three Super Bowl teams to earn a fourth ring.

GO GET A RING: BABE PARILLI

Here's what you need to know about Vito "Babe" Parilli, the Boston Patriots' starting quarterback for most of the 1960s: when Tom Brady threw his 32nd touchdown of the 2007 season, he broke a team record set by Parilli in 1964. Parilli was an outstanding member of the early Patriots. In 1968 the New York Jets traded for him to have him serve as backup and mentor to Joe Namath. The relationship worked, and Parilli finished his career with a ring from Super Bowl III.

The Pats, meanwhile, haven't exactly fallen apart without Vinatieri.

Stephen Gostkowski, a fourth-round draft pick in 2006, has been increasingly accurate on field goals—he went 20 for 26 in his rookie season and 21 for 24 in 2007—and nearly perfect on extra points, hitting all but one of his 118 PAT attempts (a record-setting 74 of which came in the '07 season). Gostkowski put up the winning points in the Patriots' 2006–07 divisional-round playoff game in San Diego, hitting a 31-yard field goal to put the Pats ahead 24–21 with 1:10 remaining. And his kickoffs have shown far more leg than Vinatieri managed in his final seasons in Foxborough.

And while the jury is still out on whether the Pats made the right move in letting Vinatieri walk away, it's worth noting that the now-35-year-old kicker's field goal accuracy dropped to 79 percent in 2007, despite the fact that he was kicking indoors.

THE BEST TRADE(S) EVER: LANDING RANDY MOSS

The Patriots went into the 2007 draft with a pair of first-round picks, their own and the one they had acquired from the Seattle Seahawks in exchange for Deion Branch. They came out with safety Brandon Merriweather, selected 24th overall, a pair of first-round choices in the 2008 draft (one of which they would later lose as part of the fallout from the Spygate incident), and arguably the best wide receiver in the NFL.

And what's amazing is that it gets even better than that. Because while the net price the Patriots paid for Randy Moss (in trade terms, not dollars) looked like nothing—literally nothing—at the time it actually turned out to be even less than that.

New England snagged Moss on day two of the draft for a fourth-round pick they'd acquired from San Francisco on day one. The fourth rounder, however, had essentially amounted to vig in a swap of first-round choices: the Patriots gave up their second 2007 first-round selection (28th overall) in exchange for the 49ers' first-round pick in 2008, with the 49ers fourth-round pick in '07 thrown in to sweeten the deal.

It would have been more than enough had the wheeling and dealing ended when the Pats shipped San Francisco's fourth-round pick to the other side of the Bay Bridge for Moss, who had worn out his welcome after two seasons in Oakland. But it didn't. The 49ers went on to finish the 2007 season with a 5–11 record, securing for the Patriots the seventh overall pick in the 2008 draft.

So in addition to landing Moss, who would become a major part of the best offense ever assembled, the Patriots ended up turning a 28th overall pick into a seventh. As this book goes to press, there's no telling what New England will do with that pick, but it's safe to guess whatever it is will work out swimmingly.

Moss certainly did.

THE WORST TRADE EVER

Okay, it's not exactly on the level of giving up the future of your franchise for a washed-up running back (see Walker, Herschel), but the Patriots did manage to trade away the opportunity to draft Jerry Rice in 1985. The Pats traded the 16th overall pick in the '85 draft, along with their third-rounder, to the 49ers (who moved up specifically to get Rice) for the 28th overall pick and San Francisco's second- and third-round picks. The Pats used San Fran's first-round pick on center Trevor Matich, who lasted four seasons in New England. Rice arguably would have been a better choice.

In his first season catching Tom Brady's passes, Moss set team and league records at an unreal clip.

Moss became the first player in NFL history to rack up 100 or more yards in his first four games with a new team. He led the team in receiving yards eight times and in receptions another eight and was twice named AFC Offensive Player of the Week and once AFC Offensive Player of the Month. He set new team single-season records for touchdowns and touchdown catches (23) and for receiving yards (1,493). And his 23 TD receptions broke a league record formerly held by Jerry Rice.

Those accomplishments went a long way to putting the lie to comments former Oakland Raiders offensive coordinator Tom Walsh had made shortly after Moss's trade to the Pats was completed.

"Randy Moss is a player whose skills are diminishing, and he's in denial of those eroding skills," Walsh told *Boston Globe* columnist Ron Borges for a May 13, 2007, column. "Randy was a great receiver, but he lacked the work ethic and the desire to cultivate any skills that would compensate for what he was losing physically later in his career."

Walsh had worked with Moss for part of the 2006 season (before he was dismissed as OC of the failing team) and had seen the receiver in his worst year as a pro. A Pro Bowl selection in five of his seven seasons with the Minnesota Vikings, Moss had cost the Raiders first- and seventh-round picks as well as linebacker Napoleon Harris in March 2005. And although it surprised no one outside of Oakland, it seemed to take the Raiders aback that the addition of one star player didn't turn their sinking ship of a franchise around overnight.

Moss suffered injuries in each of his two seasons in Oakland, which limited his production. Worse, he exhibited the attitude problem that had surfaced throughout his career any time he grew frustrated. Moss has never been a good loser. Nor has he yet done anything to distinguish himself as the kind of guy you want on your team when the chips are down (that is, in the big, "our season's going to hell and we all need to pull together" sense; he's been incredible in the "we've got to come back and pull this game out" sense).

But the Raiders were at least partially at fault for the receiver's failures. The team has been in disarray roughly since the moment Walt Coleman announced the tuck ruling in the Snow Bowl. Though they reached the Super Bowl a year later, the Raiders were already rotting from the inside, with coach Bill Callahan and players butting heads on a near-daily basis. Oakland has been cycling through head coaches and losing the majority of its games for the past five seasons.

Assuming Moss would succeed in such an environment and somehow pull the rest of the organization up with him was just another of Raiders owner Al Davis's abundant recent blunders.

Even so, Walsh wasn't the only observer Borges found willing to question the wisdom of the Moss trade in the months between the draft and the start of training camp. (It's only fair to mention that Borges, who has since resigned from the *Globe*, was routinely criticized as a Patriots hater and made no attempts to hide his obvious distaste for Bill Belichick.)

Marty Schottenheimer, whose stint as head coach of the San Diego Chargers had ended in January at the hands of the Patriots, was among the experts who claimed Moss only put in a complete effort on plays designed to get him the ball.

"When he goes full speed, you know he's the target," Schottenheimer said. "When he doesn't, you know he's not in the play."

That kind of criticism is damning for a receiver like Moss. God-given ability notwithstanding, a player like Moss can only hurt his team if he ends up giving away plays to defenses every time he's on the field.

But the Patriots were everything the Raiders weren't. Although they got Moss at a steep monetary discount—scheduled to make $9.25 million for the 2007 season in Oakland, he agreed to a one-year deal worth $5 million to move to New England—the Pats aren't a team that squanders any resources, be they free draft picks, cash, or valuable cap space, on players they know aren't cut out to succeed in their system. (Just ask Drew Bledsoe and Lawyer Milloy.) So outsiders, experts and fans alike, were forced to sit back and wait to see the product on the field, reserving judgment where they could.

It didn't take long for the Pats' investment to begin paying off. Moss developed a rapport with Brady during the off-season and in training camp. Having wowed Belichick with his physical ability years earlier (Belichick reportedly had his eye on Moss for years), he impressed the coach with his great head for the game.

"He is probably the smartest receiver I have coached," Belichick would say in a midseason press conference. "He has outstanding receiving skills. He makes great decisions on the field in terms of reading coverages and making route adjustments."

Moss had mastered the Patriots' complex offensive system by the time training camp ended. And when the team took the field for a week-one game against the New York Jets in the Meadowlands, Moss immediately set to work showing fans and the media what they could expect.

Moss caught nine passes for 183 yards and a touchdown in his first regular-season game in a Patriots uniform. His afternoon included a 51-yard touchdown that he caught in stride at the goal line with three defenders surrounding him.

By week three it was obvious that Moss hadn't lost so much as half a step. He was every bit the great wideout he had been in Minnesota. Only now he had one of the game's all-time best quarterbacks throwing the ball to him.

Moss was fast. He could stretch the field, outrun coverage, and make defenses pay for failing to pay him enough attention. He could beat tight coverage, getting up over defenders to pull down passes no one else in the league could hope to catch. He could make spectacular catches in double or triple coverage. He could make athletic, one-handed grabs while off balance and with a defender bearing down on him.

There was nothing a coach could ever ask a receiver to do that Moss couldn't handle. And there were plenty of things no one would ever ask him to do that Moss could handle anyway.

Moss's presence also made the players around him better. Defenses couldn't account for Moss without leaving openings for receivers Wes Welker, Donté Stallworth, and Jabar Gaffney, tight ends Benjamin Watson and Kyle Brady, and running backs Kevin Faulk and Laurence Maroney. And with Brady guiding the offense,

DOUBLE OOPS

Phil Olsen was the Patriots' first-round pick in the 1970 NFL draft, going fourth overall. But he never played a down for Boston. Olsen, a defensive lineman, had injured his knee in the 1970 College All-Star game (the Pats apparently didn't know) and missed the entire NFL season. A year later he took advantage of an administrative blunder—the team failed to send out the annual letter in which they informed players their options had been picked up—and left the team as a free agent. Olsen joined the Los Angeles Rams where he played defensive tackle on the same line as his brother Merlin.

leaving an opening for any player is nothing short of deadly—as every opponent the Patriots faced during the regular season would learn.

And when Jacksonville and San Diego schemed to take Moss away during the playoffs, the receiver did precisely what Schottenheimer and others said he wouldn't do: he played hard on down after down, knowing the ball probably wasn't coming his way. Moss made key blocks in both the divisional playoff win over Jacksonville and the AFC Championship victory over San Diego, paving the way for other players to achieve glory.

Up to that point there was still the possibility that Moss's critics had been right about the wideout slacking on plays designed to go to other receivers. Maybe it was just a matter of being in the Patriots' system, in which the ball can come your way on any play, that had kept Moss honest. But in the conference playoffs, Moss made it clear he was on the field to help his team win in any way he could.

The week before the Super Bowl, Moss made it clear that he wanted to keep on helping the Patriots. In his portion of the Patriots' media day press event, Moss said that although he was scheduled to hit free agency February 29 (the Pats were forbidden under the collective bargaining agreement from making a long-term deal during the season) his hope was to remain with the Patriots.

"The team concept is not just on the field, it's inside the locker room," Moss told the press. "For me to be able to say that I would love to become a New England Patriot and finish my career here...that is something that I can really believe in."

A week after the Super Bowl, Moss played in the Pro Bowl for the first time since 2003.

Call Moss the latest Patriots rehab project if you want. Or say he's a guy who recognized he had one last chance to cement his legacy and grabbed it with both hands (while jumping over a pair of DBs). Call him whatever you like. But make sure you call him the best wide receiver any team ever got for a fourth-round draft pick that wasn't theirs to begin with.

Oh, and for the record, Oakland used that pick to take cornerback John Bowie, who made his first (and only) tackle in the Raiders' last game of the season.

So that seems like a pretty fair deal.

THE SECOND-BEST TRADE EVER: WES WELKER

If in 2007 Randy Moss was the realization of every great hope the Patriots and their fans ever invested in a wide receiver—the cure for every disappointing memory of Irving Fryar and Terry Glenn, every "if only" recollection of Darryl Stingley and Hart Lee Dykes—Wes Welker was something equally important. He was the answer to the question, "What are we going to do when Troy Brown retires?" He was the workhorse-type receiver Patriots fans have always fallen in love with. The Stanley Morgan. The Gino Cappelletti. The guy who does whatever his team asks of him and who's a threat to the opposition every time he puts his hands on the ball.

Welker, who came to the Patriots by way of a March 2007 trade with the Miami Dolphins, didn't just catch more passes than Moss during the season, he caught more passes than any New England receiver ever had. His 112 receptions broke a record previously held by Brown, who snagged 101 balls in 2001.

Patriots wide receiver Wes Welker carries the ball against the Jacksonville Jaguars in the first half of an NFL divisional playoff game on January 12, 2008, in Foxborough, Massachusetts.

A three-year veteran who led all Dolphins receivers with 67 catches for 687 yards in 2006, Welker upped his yardage as well as his catch total in his first season with the Pats (those 112 receptions netted 1,175 yards). He also dramatically increased his touchdown count. Welker found the end zone eight times in 2007; he'd scored precisely one TD in his previous three seasons. And he pitched in on special teams, returning seven kickoffs for 176 yards and 25 punts for 249.

The Patriots were able to acquire Welker for relatively little in the trade with the Dolphins—New England sent Miami a second- and a seventh-round pick in the 2007 draft—largely because

Miami failed to recognize his potential. Heading into the 2007 off-season, Welker was a restricted free agent. Had Miami placed a high tender on him, promising $2 million or more in salary but ensuring that any team attempting to sign him away would have owed them at least a first-round draft choice, they might have scared the Patriots away. Instead, Miami tendered Welker at the second-round level with its lower salary offer ($1.3 million) and lower compensation level should he sign elsewhere. That allowed the Pats to make Welker an offer the Dolphins couldn't afford to match, effectively forcing Miami to the trade table. The Patriots got their man at a reasonable price; they gave him a five-year deal worth $18 million and sent their two picks south.

So how did the Pats know a guy who'd done relatively little during his first few years in the league was capable of doing so much? Simple. They'd been the victims of one of Welker's better outings.

In a 2006 meeting between the Pats and Dolphins in Foxborough, Welker had caught nine balls for 77 yards. He'd also burned them for 103 yards on four kickoff returns. The Pats won, but they learned they had to game plan for Welker.

"We couldn't handle him," Belichick said after Welker joined his team. "Couldn't tackle him, couldn't cover him, and had to double him a lot. He was a tough guy for us to match up with."

If you can't beat 'em, sign 'em.

It's a hell of a philosophy when you can make it work. And together Welker and the Patriots made it work as well as anyone might have hoped.

With Moss stretching defenses, Stallworth working intermediate routes, and Brady forever a threat to hit any receiver who gets open for a split second, Welker became a disaster waiting to happen for defenses. In one season he transitioned from a classic possession receiver, reliable underneath and sometimes dangerous, to a constant threat, a guy who could at any point in any game catch a short pass on a crossing route in heavy traffic and somehow turn it into a 20-yard gain. He became a slot receiver you had to consider double covering, not a great option when Moss and Stallworth or Gaffney are on the field.

Perhaps most important, he provided a target Tom Brady knew he could trust in the clutch; a factor that proved meaningful time and again, notably in the week-nine match between the Pats and the then-unbeaten Indianapolis Colts in the RCA Dome. Moss was the leading receiver in that much hyped game, which was tagged Super Bowl XLI½, but Welker came up big when it mattered most. With the Patriots trailing 20–10 halfway through the fourth quarter, Welker beat Colts safety Bob Sanders on a three-yard touchdown catch to bring New England to within three points. And on a crucial third-and-six just before the two-minute warning, Welker came up with a 10-yard gainer that allowed the Patriots to run out the clock and seal a 24–20 victory.

"When the game's on the line, that's who I'm throwing to," Brady said in his postgame press conference.

And there it was. With Brown on the physically-unable-to-perform list and headed for almost certain retirement, the Patriots had found their next go-to guy.

THE OTHER SECOND-BEST TRADE EVER: COREY DILLON

Corey Dillon was Randy Moss before Randy Moss was Randy Moss. At least if you're looking at things from a Patriots perspective.

During Dillon's first seven seasons in the NFL—spent with the Cincinnati Bengals, who picked him in the second round of the 1997 draft—Dillon established himself as one of the league's best running backs. But he also established a reputation as a royal pain in the patoot, a malcontent who would lash out at his teammates as easily as he would at the local and national media.

Dillon spent his time in Cincinnati setting records—at one point he owned both the rookie and overall records for rushing yards in a game—and earning Pro Bowl berths. He rushed for 7,520 yards in his first six seasons with the Bengals, racking up between 1,129 and 1,435 yards a season and putting up 43 touchdowns on the ground and another five through the air.

But Dillon didn't crave individual success. He wanted to win. And the Bengals never managed a winning season during his time in Cincinnati. The best Bengals team Dillon ever played for, in fact, was the 2003 squad, which finished 8–8, and with which he started only 11 games and rushed for only 541 yards, a result of both a groin injury and the emergence of younger running back Rudi Johnson. More often, Dillon's Bengals ended seasons with two, three, or four wins.

That didn't stop Dillon from playing hard, though, mostly because hard was the only way he knew how to play. Dillon was never a finesse player. He didn't dance around the ends or stutter-step at the line of scrimmage. He put his shoulders down and charged up the middle. If someone got in his way, he plowed through them. If they hopped on his back, he carried them along with him. When defenders tackled him, they got up feeling like they'd been the ones to take the hit.

Dillon became angry at teammates when he felt they weren't putting as much of themselves into the game as he was. He didn't like being expected to carry an entire offense on his shoulders. At one point he remarked in frustration that he'd rather "flip burgers" than keep playing for the Bengals. If fans didn't like that, Dillon didn't much care.

But Dillon also didn't seem to understand that he was alienating everyone. And when he was injured in 2003 and Cincinnati fans and new head coach Marvin Lewis went gaga for Johnson, he snapped. Dillon came to the conclusion that the team was planning to trade him. Then he started saying that he wanted a trade. Following the last game of the Bengals' season, a loss to Cleveland, Dillon threw local conventional wisdom back in the faces of fans and the media.

"They don't need me," Dillon told reporters. "They've been winning, quote unquote, without me."

The Bengals tried to work a deal with the Raiders, but it fell through when Oakland balked at giving up a second-round draft pick. The Patriots, who had just won Super Bowl XXXVIII, but who were lacking production in the running game, had no such qualms.

Dillon showed up in Foxborough ready to contribute. He embraced the Patriots' system, toned down the talk, dipped his shoulders, and ran his way to his best season. Dillon carried the ball 345 times in 2004, gaining 1,625 yards and scoring 12 touchdowns.

Dillon drew nothing but praise from his Patriots teammates.

And he earned his Super Bowl XXXIX ring, cranking out 75 yards and a touchdown on 18 carries, plus an additional 31 yards on three catches, against a stout Philadelphia Eagles defense.

When Dillon asked the Patriots to release him following the 2006 season, he left the game having 11,241 career yards and 82 rushing touchdowns, placing him 14th on the league's all-time rushing list. Those numbers, combined with the ring he earned in New England, make him a safe bet for enshrinement in the Pro Football Hall of Fame.

Maybe you could never prove it by Al Davis, but that's pretty good value for a second-round pick.

OWNERSHIP: FROM BAD TO WORSE TO WEIRDEST TO BEST

FOUNDERING FATHERS: THE SULLIVANS

It can be hard to make your peace with Billy Sullivan and his sons, Chuck and Pat. Especially now that Patriots fans have seen what a serious team owner can do for a franchise.

In many ways the Robert Kraft era has made it harder than ever to forgive the Sullivans for the decades of turmoil they foisted on New England football fans through cheapness and ineptitude. But there's also one stubborn fact you can never ignore: without Billy Sullivan there would be no New England Patriots.

That has to count for something.

Sullivan wasn't the first person to bring professional football to the city where American football was invented. He was the seventh. And none of the six teams to take up residence in the Hub before Sullivan came along had succeeded.

The Boston Bulldogs of the original American Football League lasted a season. The second team to be called the Bulldogs, an NFL franchise previously known as the Pottsville Maroons (famous for their claim to the disputed 1925 NFL championship), also hung around for a single season. The Boston Braves/Redskins spent five seasons in town before relocating to Washington. The Boston Shamrocks survived for two years and brought home the second AFL's championship in 1936. The Boston Bears, of the third AFL, lasted only a season. And the NFL's Boston Yanks played five seasons in town before shipping off to New York in 1949.

PAT SULLIVAN VS. THE L.A. RAIDERS

Because it would have been an affront to the football gods for anything good to happen to the Sullivan-era Patriots without some kind of insanity taking place on the side, Pat Sullivan found himself in a brawl with a pair of Los Angeles Raiders players during the 1985 playoffs. The Pats had beaten L.A. (en route to their first Super Bowl), when Sullivan became involved in a sideline argument with Raiders defensive end Howie Long. When Sullivan grabbed Long's facemask, linebacker Matt Millen jumped in, swung his helmet, and took a chunk out of Pat's cranium. The Pats GM took eight stitches.

It's no mystery, then, why the NFL told Sullivan it wasn't interested when he looked into bringing a new franchise to Boston in 1959.

But the former sportswriter and PR man for Boston College, Notre Dame, and the Boston Braves (baseball variety), wanted to be in the professional football business. And when he learned that Lamar Hunt was looking for an eighth franchise for his newly created American Football League, Sullivan found nine friends to join him in ponying up $25,000 each, raised another $250,000 through the sale of nonvoting stock, and created the Boston Patriots.

By all accounts Sullivan was a mostly amiable man. And he was typical of the original AFL franchise owners in that he became involved for love of the game rather than for a love of money.

Trouble was, unlike Hunt, Bud Adams, Barron Hilton, and other members of the so-called Foolish Club, Sullivan was anything but a wealthy man. Having founded the Patriots, he had little money left to operate the team.

That put the Pats at a competitive disadvantage early on. While other AFL owners could at least try to lure top college prospects away from the more established NFL by offering better compensation, Sullivan's Patriots generally were left to work with players the older league's teams didn't want.

That didn't cripple the team. The Pats were able to rescue talented players like Gino Cappelletti and Jim Colclough from the Canadian Football League. They were also able to sign players overlooked by the NFL and to occasionally come out on top when they competed with a player who attracted minor interest from an NFL team. But when the stakes were high, the Patriots typically lost. (As when quarterback Jack Concannon, the Pats' first overall pick in the 1964 AFL draft, opted for the Philadelphia Eagles' $50,000 offer over the Pats' $25,000.)

Worse still, when Sullivan did reach for his wallet, he usually ended up getting bit on the rear end. In 1970 the Patriots made quarterback Joe Kapp the highest-paid player in football at $130,000. A Pro Bowl player who had led Minnesota to Super Bowl IV a year earlier, Kapp stunk up the field in Boston, completing 98 of 219 passes for 1,104 yards and a ridiculous three touchdowns. On the eve of the 1971 season, Kapp announced he was unhappy with his contract and retired from football. No one in Boston was sad to see him go, least of all the owner who had so grossly overpaid him.

In reality it was partly because of Sullivan's insistence on running his team as economically as possible that the Pats survived the early years of the AFL. But as the league grew stronger, then merged with the NFL, and the revenues grew more abundant, Sullivan never changed his approach. That created problems with players, who felt they were nickeled and dimed on every contract and were sometimes made financial promises it later became clear Sullivan had no intention of keeping.

Sullivan's tightness with a buck also had a way of hampering the franchise's popularity.

As if it weren't difficult enough to support a team that consistently fell short on the field, Pats fans were asked, beginning in 1971, to trek to Foxborough to watch games in Sullivan's new Schaefer Stadium. Fans were excited by the fact that the team had a home of its own after 11 gypsy seasons that had seen the Pats play in every stadium, park, and oversized backyard in Boston. But Foxborough?

The town Sullivan had chosen as home to his team sat 30 miles outside of Boston. It was close to nowhere. And Route 1, the two-lane state road on which Schaefer Stadium was located, was in no way suited to support the traffic generated by the arrival of 60,000 fans within a few hours on Sunday afternoons, making the site virtually impossible to reach.

Worse still, if you managed to make it to Schaefer, you usually ended up wishing you hadn't. Built on the cheap, the stadium featured aluminum benches that would sear your flesh early in the season and send a deep freeze up through your intestinal system come December. The seat numbers painted on the benches were largely ignored. And the space allotted to each ticket holder was Lilliputian. The stadium's toilets didn't work right, resulting in a horrible stench that made bathrooms unapproachable by halftime of any halfway well-attended game. And you couldn't walk through the concourse without wondering at what point the whole place was going to collapse and bury you alive.

That didn't do much to promote team spirit in the region. And in years when the team was bad, it became too easy to stay home and watch the Giants, Steelers, or Raiders on TV (Patriots games were never on, because they were never sold out).

The stadium alienated fans. Billy Sullivan and his eldest son, Chuck, alienated coaches and players.

In addition to Kapp's walkout, the 1971 preseason saw defensive lineman Phil Olsen, the team's first-round pick in the 1970 draft, walk away after an administrative error made every player on the team a free agent. Olsen, who never played a snap for the Patriots, signed with the Los Angeles Rams for more than the Patriots were willing to give him.

John Hannah, the future Hall of Fame guard, tussled with the Sullivans over money constantly and publicly. Hannah felt Billy and Chuck tried to set him up with a game of good cop/bad cop over a deal he and Leon Gray had hammered out with coach Chuck Fairbanks prior to the 1977 season. That fight led to a three-game holdout. Fairbanks's departure from the team a year later was complicated by Billy's decision to suspend the coach after he learned he'd made arrangements to take a job running the University of Colorado's football team beginning in 1979. By the time Sullivan unsuspended Fairbanks for the playoffs, the team was in disarray—and a Patriots squad that might have contended dropped out of the playoffs in the first round.

It seemed like every year it was something. A bad coaching move. A foolish trade. Just when fans would start to think the Patriots might be coming around, the Sullivans would find a way to pull the rug out from under their team.

Fans watched the never-ending circus, shook their heads, and wondered what it would be like to follow a real NFL franchise.

There was a glimmer of hope when Pat Sullivan assumed the job of general manager in 1983. Pat knew more about football than his father. (And everybody knew more about football than Chuck.) He started roughly, though, hardballing Mike Haynes out of town. And while he at least received a first-round pick from Los Angeles for the future Hall of Fame cornerback, he preceded to blow that pick, trading up to take troubled wide receiver Irving Fryar in the 1984 draft. Pat did hire Raymond Berry to take over as head coach that year, though, so he has one good decision to his credit.

The Sullivans' constant struggles with finances finally caught up to them. In 1984 Chuck decided to turn himself into a concert-industry mogul. He made a deal to promote the Jacksons' (as in

ST. LOUIS'S THIRD CHOICE

By the time it became clear that James Orthwein would not be able to move the Patriots to St. Louis, Orthwein's partners back home already had begun discussions with the Los Angeles Rams. And in 1995 the Rams made the leap from Anaheim to the Gateway City. St. Louis's second and third choices to be its representative in the NFL would meet six years later in Super Bowl XXXVI.

Michael, Tito, Jermaine, and the others) Victory Tour, sinking millions of dollars he didn't have into the venture. Chuck miscalculated the potential profitability of the tour and ended up losing his shirt. Or actually it was his father's shirt.

With the debt Chuck had taken on in the concert business, and the money the Sullivans already owed to various note holders and investors in the team and stadium, the family ended up $120 million in the hole. They lost their stadium in bankruptcy proceedings, during which it was purchased by Boston businessman and Patriots fan Robert Kraft. (Kraft quickly changed the name of the building from Sullivan Stadium—which it had taken on after Schaefer Brewing's naming rights contract expired in 1983—to Foxboro Stadium.) And, after the league refused to allow him to sell nonvoting shares in the team to the public to raise funds, Billy was forced to put the Pats on the market. In 1988, Sullivan reached an agreement to sell the franchise to electric shaver magnate Victor Kiam for $84 million.

The Sullivans were out of the picture as owners, though Billy stayed on as president and Pat as general manager, and there was hope among fans. But that hope proved fleeting.

MIDDLEMEN: VICTOR KIAM AND JAMES ORTHWEIN

It was as if some omnipotent personage somewhere had a point to make. And the point went something like this: You think the Sullivans were bad? The Sullivans were a dream. I'll show you what bad looks like.

And voila. There was Victor Kiam, $84 million in personal grooming profits burning a hole in his pocket, ready to step in and rescue the New England Patriots.

For all his faults, Billy Sullivan had approached the Patriots as a labor of love. Sullivan started the team in a town that had never supported professional football and at a time when even the NFL's team owners, a group with a significant stake in the growth potential of the sport, didn't believe there was room in Americans' hearts for more than a dozen pro teams. He had built the team and helped build the AFL into an entity the older league couldn't ignore. And he had seen the team through most of three decades of sometimes painful growth.

Kiam, who was able to gain a majority stake in the team only because the alternative for Sullivan was financial ruin, saw the Patriots as a sort of trophy.

Kiam had grown rich through the success of his company, Remington Products, a manufacturer of electric shavers, razor blades, and other personal grooming gear. (Kiam was the guy who liked the electric shaver so much he bought the company.) He was taken with his own wealth and success—he even wrote a book bragging about what a smart businessman he was—and he saw owning an NFL team as the perfect status symbol, a traveling, televised tribute to his keen business acumen.

Thus, when he had the chance to partner with Philadelphia businessman Fran Murray, who owned an option to buy the Patriots from Sullivan and was trying to force a deal, Kiam decided quickly that he wanted in. Kiam bankrolled the deal and started living out his four-star daydream ("think I'll buy me a football team").

Victor Kiam's (right) tenure as Patriots owner is remembered as one of the worst periods in team history.

Owning the Patriots turned out to be less of a dream than Kiam probably imagined.

To begin with, it didn't take long to discover that a lot of the money in professional sports comes from stadium revenues. And Kiam didn't own a stadium. The building his team played in belonged to Robert Kraft, who'd bought it in a bankruptcy auction. Kraft also controlled the land around the stadium—you know, the land people paid to park on when they went to a game. Kiam owned the team, but Kraft, for all intents and purposes, owned Kiam.

And the team, for most of the years Kiam was in place, hardly seemed worth owning. The Pats didn't do anything right on the field. The team won nine games in 1988 and 12 more the next three years. In 1990 Kiam put himself in the middle of a national firestorm with his gross mishandling of the Lisa Olson incident. And his team was spiraling out of control, with players fighting in bars and being arrested on weapons charges. The team posted a franchise-worst 1–15 record that season, and Kiam became ever more visibly miserable.

When Murray decided he'd had enough following the 1991 season and wanted out, Kiam couldn't afford the buyout. He was forced to sell his share of the team to James Busch Orthwein, a businessman from St. Louis.

Things were a bit weird under Orthwein, but for the most part they started looking up.

Orthwein never wanted to be the owner of the New England Patriots. What he wanted was to be involved with bringing an expansion team to his native St. Louis, where his family had achieved a certain level of success in the brewing business (that's Busch as in Anheuser-Busch).

The St. Louis Cardinals had pulled up stakes for drier pastures in Arizona in 1988, and Orthwein was part of a group that had been trying to secure a replacement. He purchased the Patriots when the chance arose, figuring he could move the team to Missouri if the expansion deal didn't work out.

Orthwein began preparing the Pats for the eventual move by steering them back toward respectability. He fired coach Dick

McPherson, who'd managed eight wins in two seasons, and brought in Bill Parcells, the Super Bowl-winning former coach of the New York Giants. If Orthwein was going to import a team to St. Louis, it wasn't going to be the hopeless perpetual loser of a squad he had wrested from Kiam. And Parcells was perhaps the only coach on the market at the time who could restore a team's credibility just by walking in the front door.

In the fall of 1993, the NFL denied the St. Louis group's bid for an expansion franchise, choosing instead to take its product to Charlotte and Jacksonville. The Pats finished the season 5–11. And reports circulated that the team would soon be packing its bag and heading west.

But it wasn't that easy. Like Kiam before him, Orthwein had failed to take Kraft into account. And as it had been for Kiam, that proved to be a mistake.

Kraft had the team locked into a lease it couldn't hope to break. Orthwein couldn't leave town without effectively bankrupting the franchise.

Orthwein offered Kraft $75 million to buy the Pats out of their obligation, but Kraft refused, instead telling Orthwein he was interested in purchasing the team.

Orthwein was unhappy, but he was beaten. And his cohorts in St. Louis had already identified another franchise that was ready to find a new home and able to move without becoming insolvent. So he sold the team to Kraft for $172 million, then the largest sum paid for a professional sports organization, and went home. The Kraft era, and everything it would bring to New England, was officially under way.

THE REAL DEAL: ROBERT KRAFT

It's tempting, and not uncommon, to apply a certain revisionist romanticism to the Robert Kraft era. With the Patriots in great distress, our hero Sir Robert arrives in Foxborough armed with a bag full of cash, vanquishes the dread villain Kiam, and thwarts Lord Orthwein's plans to plunder New England's treasured team, ushering in a Golden Age in Patriots Nation.

Thing is—not so much.

Oh, sure, Kraft was the best owner in team history from the second he and Orthwein completed their deal in 1994. Kraft is a rarity, a devoted fan who realized his dream of one day owning his favorite team, and he's been a godsend for football fans in New England. But it's not as if Kraft stepped in to the owners box and the Patriots immediately commenced winning Super Bowls.

Indeed, while the Patriots did make the playoffs for the first time in eight years during their first season under Kraft's ownership, that accomplishment had considerably more to do with Bill Parcells than it did with his new boss. And, either way, the Pats took a step back a year later, finishing the 1995 season with a record of 6–10. For a while it appeared it didn't matter how good or bad the team's owner or coach were, the Patriots were just one of those teams that would never get over the hump.

Current Patriots owner Robert Kraft, widely acknowledged as the best owner in Patriots history, is essentially an avid fan who had the means to buy his favorite team.

That changed in 1996 as the team powered its way to an 11–5 record, qualified for the playoffs, and charged to a berth in Super Bowl XXXI.

But on the inside, things weren't so grand. Kraft and Parcells clashed. The coach had been promised control over the team by Orthwein, an owner who was never much interested in being involved with the day-to-day operations of the organization. Under Kraft, however, Parcells's decisions were subject to a certain level of scrutiny. Kraft wasn't an Al Davis or Jerry Jones type who wanted to coach his team from the owner's box, but he was a highly successful businessman with ideas about financial matters—ideas that were becoming more important in the then-new salary-cap era—and who expected to be heard.

The battle of wills between owner and coach brought out the worst in both men. Kraft, after overruling Parcells's wishes and insisting that the team draft Terry Glenn with the seventh pick in the 1996 draft, boasted openly that there was "a new sheriff in town." Parcells took out his frustrations on the rookie, gave Kraft the silent treatment, and in the end spent time scheming to defect to the New York Jets when he should have been game planning to face the Green Bay Packers in the Super Bowl.

When things finally fell apart, with Parcells ditching his team before the champagne had popped in Green Bay's locker room, Kraft made yet another bad decision. Though he recognized that the best choice to succeed Parcells was the Tuna's assistant head coach, Bill Belichick, he let his anger at Parcells cloud his judgment. Wanting the bad taste of the Parcells experiment out of his mouth, Kraft turned to Pete Carroll, the San Francisco 49ers' defensive coordinator who'd had an unsuccessful one-year stint as head coach of the Jets.

Three years later, after watching Carroll's easygoing "players' coach" approach produce ever-less-satisfying results, Kraft finally brought in Belichick—at the cost of a first round draft pick surrendered to the rival Jets.

It was then—or really a year later, when Belichick found the right quarterback for his offensive system—that the Golden Age truly began.

Of course, the Golden Age was very nearly centered not in Foxborough but in Hartford, Connecticut.

Kraft knew the Patriots needed a new stadium even in the days when he was merely the team's landlord. Foxboro Stadium had been a substandard facility when it was built in 1971. And when Kraft purchased it from the Sullivan family in 1988, it was by far the worst stadium in professional football (and probably in all of professional sports).

But after running into difficulties with his various proposals to build a new home for the team, both in Boston and in Foxborough, Kraft all but gave up on the idea of keeping the Patriots in Massachusetts. He considered Providence as a new home, but that was going nowhere. And then the state of Connecticut came along with an offer Kraft couldn't refuse. Rather than having to spend his own money to build a new stadium, Kraft could relocate the Patriots to Hartford, where the taxpayers would put the Pats up in a beautiful new $300 million, 68,000-seat facility.

Kraft signed an agreement and started making plans for the move. Then he thought better of it. Even if it weren't for the sentimental attachments to Foxborough, there seemed little wisdom in moving the team even farther away from New England's largest and most prosperous city. Connecticut had guaranteed 30 years of sellouts, but the guarantee was about revenue, not fan base. And Kraft recognized that in leaving Massachusetts, he'd be walking away from the area that was home to a high concentration of Patriots fans—not to mention making the team even less accessible for fans in much of Rhode Island and the northern New England states.

The Patriots backed out of their agreement to move to Connecticut, and Kraft set about securing financing for a $325 million stadium project in Foxborough. He also signed notes promising to repay the Commonwealth for more than $60 million in infrastructure improvements. Not only would Kraft have a new stadium for the 2002 season, but the stadium would also be easily accessible to the fans.

Best yet, Kraft's new facility would play host to a team fans would want to come out and see. The Snow Bowl game, in which the Patriots prevailed over the Oakland Raiders to move forward in the 2001–02 playoffs, would be the last contest ever to take place in Foxboro Stadium, ensuring that fans' final memories of the old building, if few others, would be positive.

Two weeks after that sendoff, Kraft stood on stage in New Orleans with presenter Terry Bradshaw and NFL Commissioner Paul Tagliabue, raised the Lombardi Trophy over his head and declared, "Today, everyone in America is a Patriot, and the Patriots are world champions." A new era was beginning.

The gates of Gillette Stadium swung open on September 9, 2002, with the Patriots hosting the Pittsburgh Steelers in a rematch of the 2001–02 AFC Championship. The Pats were defending champs for the first time in their history. They had a coach who had engineered one of the most stunning upset victories in Super Bowl history (two if you counted the one he'd masterminded 11 years earlier as defensive coordinator for the New York Giants). They had a promising young quarterback. They had an owner who knew he could trust his coach and his front office to build and maintain a great team. And they had a home that was quite possibly the best facility in the National Football League.

The Golden Age of the New England Patriots was officially under way. Camelot was open for business.

SOURCES

Anderson, Dave. "Has O'Brien Lost Nerve?" *The New York Times*, November 13, 1989.

Araton, Harvey. "Parcells Has Mirer, and Doubts." *The New York Times*, September 14, 1999.

Associated Press, "Fate Trips Up Dykes One More Time," May 11, 1993.

Associated Press, "Bledsoe's Return Sparks Patriots Past Steelers 24–17," January 27, 2002.

Battista, Judy. "Patriots Hire Belichick, and Everyone's Happy." *The New York Times*, January 28, 2000.

Battista, Judy. "Kicking With the Enemy: Vinatieri Is Embraced by the Colts." *The New York Times*, September 3, 2006.

Borges, Ron. "Fuzzy Math." *Pro Football Weekly*, March 26, 2001.

Borges, Ron. "Branch Not Reporting to Camp." *The Boston Globe*, July 26, 2006.

Bruschi, Tedy and Michael Holley. *Never Give Up: My Stroke, My Recovery & My Return to the NFL*. Hoboken, New Jersey: Wiley, 2007.

Cafardo, Nick. "Brady Inspires Tough Love." *The Boston Globe*, September 25, 2003.

Chicago Sun-Times, "Pats Receiver Fryar Arrested," February 16, 1988.

Clayton, John. "Giants in the Mix, but Five Others Might Be Stronger," ESPN.com, February 5, 2008.

CNNSI.com, "Bills Acquire QB Bledsoe From Patriots," April 21, 2002.

Eskenazi, Gerald. "Reluctant Eason Reports to Jets," *The New York Times*, November 9, 1989.

Eskenazi, Gerald. "Parcells Isn't Telling the No. 1 Secret," *The New York Times*, April 22, 1993.

Eskenazi, Gerald. "Belichick Solution Is Probably Close By," *The New York Times*, January 9, 2000.

Farley, Glenn. "The 1985 Patriots' Historic Journey to the Franchise's First Ever Super Bowl," Patriots.com, August 7, 2005.

Farley, Glenn. "Spirit of '76," Patriots.com, February 9, 2007.

Felger, Michael. *Tales From the Patriots Sideline*. Champaign, Illinois: Sports Publishing, 2004.

Gasper, Christopher L. "Belichick Looks Ahead," *The Boston Globe*, February 6, 2008.

George, Thomas. "Patriots and 3 Players Fined in Olson Incident." *The New York Times*, November 28, 1990.

Halberstam, David. *The Education of a Coach*. New York, New York: Hyperion, 2005.

Honolulu Star-Bulletin. "Pats Edwards Might be Lost for '99," February 6, 1999.

Holley, Michael. *Patriot Reign*. New York, New York: William Morrow, 2004.

Janofsky, Michael. "Holdout Defenders Not Missed So Far," *The New York Times*, September 30, 1983.

Lee, Robert. "Versatile Troy Brown Is Ready to Roll," *Providence Journal*, November 30, 2007.

Litsky, Frank. "Billy Sullivan, 86, Founder of Football Patriots, Dies." *The New York Times*, February 24, 1998.

MacMullan, Jackie. "Vinatieri Shunned Patriots." *The Boston Globe*, August 10, 2006.

McManaman, Bob. "Welker Comes up Big for Pats." *The Arizona Republic*, January 26, 2008.

Paolantonio, Sal, with Reuben Frank. *The Paolantonio Report*. Chicago, Illinois: Triumph Books, 2007.

Patriots Insider.com. "Patriots' Bruschi Returns to Practice," October 19, 2005.

Pierces, Charles P. *Moving the Chains: Tom Brady and the Pursuit of Everything*. New York, New York: Farrar, Straus and Giroux, 2007.

Price, Christopher. *The Blueprint*. New York, New York: Thomas M. Dunne Books, 2007.

Reiss, Mike. "Teammates Got a Kick Out of Flutie's Drop." *The Boston Globe*, January 2, 2006.

Reiss, Mike and Christopher L. Gasper. "Catching Ultimate Compliment." *The Boston Globe*, October 25, 20007.

Ricchiardi, Sherry. "Offensive Interference." *American Journalism Review*, December/January 2005.

Richmond, Peter. "Grace After the Fall." *The New York Times*, December 30, 2007.

Smith, Michael. "Sources: Patriots Give Belichick Long-Term Extension." ESPN.com, September 17, 2007.

Sports Business.com, "Patriots Sign Deal to Move to Hartford," September 27, 2001.

Time Magazine. "Sunshine Patriots," August 16, 1971.

Tomase, John. "NFL Apology Colt Comfort for Hobbs." *Boston Herald*, July 28, 2007.

USA Today, "Spygate a 'Pandora's Box' for NFL," January 29, 2008.

Waszak, Dennis Jr. "Pats' Bruschi Inspires Stroke Survivors." Associated Press, January 28, 2008.

Whitaker, Leslie. "Trouble in the Locker Rooms." *Time Magazine*, October 15, 1990.

Zimmerman, Paul. "A Brilliant Case for the Defense." *Sports Illustrated*, February 3, 1986.